Crash Course in Library Services for Seniors

**Recent Titles in
Libraries Unlimited Crash Course Series**

Crash Course in Library Services for Seniors

Ann Roberts and Stephanie G. Bauman

Crash Course Series

LIBRARIES UNLIMITED

AN IMPRINT OF ABC-CLIO, LLC
Santa Barbara, California • Denver, Colorado • Oxford, England

Copyright 2012 by Ann Roberts and Stephanie G. Bauman

Library of Congress Cataloging-in-Publication Data

Roberts, Elizabeth Ann.
   Crash course in library services for seniors / Ann Roberts and Stephanie G. Bauman.
     pages cm. — (Crash course series)
   Includes bibliographical references and index.
   ISBN 978-1-61069-079-9 (pbk.) — ISBN 978-1-61069-080-5 (ebook)
1. Libraries and older people.   I. Bauman, Stephanie G.   II. Title.
   Z711.92.A35R63   2012
   027.62'2—dc23   2012009358

ISBN: 978-1-61069-079-9
EISBN: 978-1-61069-080-5

16 15 14 13 12   1 2 3 4 5

This book is also available on the World Wide Web as an eBook.
Visit www.abc-clio.com for details.

Libraries Unlimited
An Imprint of ABC-CLIO, LLC

ABC-CLIO, LLC
130 Cremona Drive, P.O. Box 1911
Santa Barbara, California 93116-1911

This book is printed on acid-free paper (∞)

Manufactured in the United States of America

Appendix A: American Library Association's "Guidelines for Library and Information
Services to Older Adults" are reprinted with permission of the Reference and User
Services Association (RUSA), a division of the American Library Association (ALA),
www.ala.org/rusa.

CONTENTS

INTRODUCTION

Never has it been a better time to promote services for seniors at your library. With all the rapid changes in information technology, seniors are frequently left behind and may not even know where to go to find the information they need. For years, seniors have supported, and continue to support, their local libraries through volunteering, attending programs, and tax levies. While libraries have traditionally offered programming geared toward older adults, with the downturn in the economy, rapidly changing advances in technology, and the sudden boom in senior populations, it is more important than ever to offer programs and services to meet the needs of this rapidly expanding population. Involving and engaging seniors not only offers a great service to your community, but also demonstrates that libraries are worth their vote at the election polls, and there are few libraries that don't need that vote of support. With ever-increasing demands on our libraries' resources, it becomes even more difficult to keep providing specialized services to the many demographics in our communities. For this reason, we have endeavored to gather the tools you will need to provide a higher level of service to this deserving portion of the population and create an effective but simple senior program at your library. This book offers a firm foundation for addressing the specific needs of seniors as a unique population, a clear plan for creating a dedicated space, a list of top-notch services, tips and outlines for creating innovative programming, as well as evaluation and marketing techniques.

When we imagine the ideal scenario for seniors to encounter when they go to their local public library, well . . . we dream big. We like to imagine seniors finding a dedicated service area staffed with trained librarians to meet their needs, a customized collection, and top-of-the-line services and programming. However, under the heading of "Reality Check" we realize that grand imagining doesn't always mesh with the realities of a library's size, budget, access, staffing, and so on. In this book, written by a bona fide baby boomer and a recent masters of library science (MLS) graduate with a fresh eye toward programming, we decided to shoot for the moon and include so many great ideas that you'll find it easy to pick and choose those that work best for creating your own amazing set of programs and services customized to meet the needs of your library. Of course, if we allow ourselves to dream big, and couple those dreams with hard work and dedication, we sometimes find our dreams coming true!

CHAPTER 1

Why Single Out Seniors?

Today's older adults are a "seize the day" generation. They have had access to health care, education, and career opportunities, not to mention that they have witnessed a world of change and history making. They really know what it means to work hard and to have the world as their oyster! Living longer and healthier has allowed the seniors of today to continue their life explorations and contributions through second careers, interests and hobbies, and volunteering. They are curious, enthusiastic, and interested in finding out what is just around the corner for them. As librarians, we can be a core part of the excitement.

So why do older adults have needs that differ from the general adult population? How will the current wave of baby boomers change things? Furthermore, how will the increasing growth of this segment of the population affect our library services in the coming years? Baby boomers, born between 1946 and 1964, started turning 65 in 2011, and thereafter the number considered the older population will grow from 35 million in 2000 to 71.5 million in 2030 (Federal Interagency Forum on Aging-Related Statistics, 2008). In the future, the median age of the population will be older than it is now, increasing from 34.0 in 1994 to 35.5 in 2000, and it will peak at 39.1 in 2035 (Day, 2011).

With statistics like this, it seems that no one can ignore the impact of our aging population. In the last few years, it has become increasingly evident that librarians need to work harder to meet the demands of this growing, and diverse, aging population through innovative programming and services. As the population of seniors is growing by leaps and bounds, more librarians are realizing that they need to step up or even start up services for this underserved population. A 2007 survey conducted by the librarians of the Free Library of Philadelphia system discovered that only 1 percent of their 3,500 programs were designated for seniors (Cornog, McPeak, and Ray, 2010). This statistic only serves to remind us what an underserved and rapidly growing population we are considering here.

ALA GUIDELINES FOR LIBRARY AND INFORMATION SERVICES TO OLDER ADULTS

Since the 1970s, the national professional organization for librarians, the American Library Association (ALA), has had a longstanding record of promoting library and information services to older adults. During the 1970s, members considered older adults important enough to have developed specific guidelines for serving this portion of the population. Created by the Library Services to an Aging Population Committee, Reference Services Section, Reference and User Services Association of the American Library Association in 1987, these guidelines, revised in 1999 and approved in 2008, offer a standard of service to older adults.

The American Library Association's guidelines have been updated to respond to the changing demographics of an aging U.S. population. The updating of these guidelines began in 2005. Current and past members of the Library Services to an Aging Population Committee and the Office of Literacy and Outreach Services (OLOS) Library Service to the Aging Subcommittee contributed to this revision.

Guidelines for Library and Information Services to Older Adults

The guidelines, in their entirety, can be found in Appendix A, but here are a few of the features upon which we have based some of our own suggestions:

- Acquire current data about the older population and incorporate it into planning and budgeting.
- Involve older adults in the library's planning process by establishing an advisory committee. This committee might include older adults who are regular library users; library volunteers, staff, board members, or members of the library's Friends group; and leaders of organizations of older adults and other community organizations.
- Consider how the library can be made more visible, more welcoming, and more relevant to older adult users.
- Establish an ongoing liaison with agencies that serve older adults (especially senior centers that employ activity coordinators) to explore cooperative programming, recruit volunteers or friends of the library, and seek suggestions for programs or services that would encourage library use.
- Make the library's collections and physical facilities safe, comfortable and inviting for all older adults.
- Accommodate users for whom prolonged standing is difficult by placing chairs or stools near stacks, information desks, check-out areas, computer terminals, and other areas. If possible, create a "Senior Space," using easy chairs gathered in an area adjacent to books and magazines of interest to older adults.
- Make the library a focal point for information services to older adults.
- Consider developing or expanding the library's website to provide links to the sites of organizations of older adults, government departments and agencies serving older adults, newspapers and other websites whose focus is older adults.
- Target the older population in library programming.
- Plan programs each year that specifically target older adults and enhance their ability to remain independent and skillful library users. Publicizing such programs can heighten the library's visibility among the older population.

The guidelines in part here and in their entirety in Appendix A are reprinted with permission of the Reference and User Services Association (RUSA), a division of the ALA, www.ala.org/rusa.

ONE SIZE FITS ALL?

Can seniors, as a group, fall into a "one size fits all" category for information needs and programming? The answer to that question is both yes and no. It is fairly simple to create a standard plan for children and teens, as they are going through very similar emotional, social, and physical changes within a set time frame, but the same cannot be held true for the senior population. While they are going through changes as well, these are often far more gradual, spaced over 20 to 30 years or more, and each person is going though different changes at different times and at different rates. While the older population is as varied as the rest of the adult population in many ways, many of them do have a shared set of information needs at certain stages of their later lives.

People approaching retirement obviously have many questions about retirement possibilities. Where should we live? Should we sell our home and relocate? Some would-be retirees are also thinking about finding new employment after retirement because they can't afford to be fully retired. Therefore, many seniors have the need for job-skills development or job-searching assistance. Baby boomers might wish to retire but need to stay in the workforce longer because of financial reasons or the raising of the retirement age as suggested by the government. The recent and lingering financial crisis will also contribute greatly to this trend (Williamson, Bannister, Sullivan, 2010, p. 180).

AGING AS A STATE OF MIND

In *The Secret Life of the Grown-Up Brain: The Surprising Talents of the Middle-Aged Mind*, Barbara Strauch begins her book with amusing anecdotes of forgetfulness that many of us can recognize—losing one's car keys, losing one's car in the parking lot, finding things in odd places, forgetting names, and so on—but Strauch goes on to explain that some of these changes in our *memory* are dictated by changes in our *brains*. While everyone acknowledges that our brains do slow down with age, Strauch suggests that our brains merely change with age and not necessarily for the worse. While reactions slow down and mental processes take more time, an older brain is capable of deeper and richer thought processes, and a slower reaction time also means slower to react in anger or in deed. Portions of the brain that respond to stress and fear, accounting for the fight-or-flight response, become less functional, creating a calmer outlook on life. An older adult has a greater vocabulary than a younger person, as we never stop learning new words, and older adults, through the simple physiology of the workings of the brain, gain a greater understanding of themselves and the world—hence, the wisdom of old age.

According to Strauch, new research suggests that many accepted notions about the aging brain are myths, particularly in reference to middle-aged brains and the aging brain in general. While not all these myths apply to every part of the aging population, these are widely accepted notions about the aging brain that have come under scrutiny by the scientific community and have recently been repudiated by the same.

COMMON MYTHS ABOUT OUR AGING BRAINS

- Brain cells die as we age.

For many years, it was a commonly held belief that brain cells died as we aged, but new brain-scanning technology shows that healthy individuals keep most of their brain cells for their entire lifespan.

- Our brains stop developing in our 20s.

Our brains continue to develop and change throughout our lives, allowing us to make better judgments and find unique solutions to problems, something scientists call cognitive expertise. Cognitive expertise actually peaks in middle age, a time when other faculties ("Where'd I put the car keys?") begin to slow down. Evidence also shows that we become more creative as we get older.

- Our brains start to fade away.

On the contrary, middle-aged brains begin to use two parts of the brain instead of one to solve problems, creating a boost in brain power and sometimes arriving at conclusions less quickly than their younger counterparts but with a more "thoughtful" conclusion. People with greater education and higher cognitive abilities learn to use their brains this way.

- Dementia is inevitable.

While dementia will affect some older adults, we now have more people living long enough to show that dementia is not inevitable. Increasing numbers of people maintain their faculties well into their 90s.

- We can do nothing to improve our brains.

Increasing evidence shows that exercise, education, and even what we eat can and does make a difference in how we age.

It is wonderful to know that even though younger brains might respond faster than older ones, the older brains, when healthy, can still come up with the same answers or even better answers than their younger counterparts; it just takes a bit longer due to the usage of different parts of the brain in older adults. So there's no denying that older adults are different in many ways, not only because of physical changes, but due to changes in the brain, as well. However, these changes may not be as great as some believe.

In *The Mature Mind: The Positive Power of the Aging Brain*, Dr. Gene D. Cohen talks about four phases older adults go through. Phase I is midlife reevaluation, in which we start to wonder about how many years we really have left. Pondering the years ahead as well as the years behind us frequently causes people to reevaluate what they have or have not done thus far. Such reevaluation is frequently the springboard for a second career, a new hobby, or the serious pursuit of something we might have dabbled with in younger years but failed to pursue wholeheartedly.

Phase II is a liberation phase, a phase in which we tend to think, "If I don't do it now, when?" and jump into new endeavors without fear. This new fearlessness spurs people to accomplish what the reevaluation period has made them feel they should pursue. In the liberation phase, people might become politically or socially active, finally taking a stand for what they might have quietly believed in all their lives.

Phase III is a summing up phase. Older people tend to wonder about family history or want to share some of their life's story. Cohen suggests that the usage of both sides of the brain at this point in life brings about a deeper recall of life's events and that the brain relishes the chance to see things in this different light. Things that might have been traumatic at the time seem less so now.

Phase IV is the encore phase, which should not be viewed as the swan song, but rather as the continuation of the themes we have created throughout our lives. If the body is weaker in many older people, the spirit becomes stronger as a means of compensation. In the encore phase, people frequently feel spiritually stronger and more connected to family and friends than ever and will continue to engage in their interests, even if in a different way.

FACTORS ASSOCIATED WITH LONGEVITY AND GOOD HEALTH

In *Boomers and Beyond: Reconsidering the Role of Libraries,* edited by Pauline Rothstein and Diantha Dow Schull (2010), we find some suggested protective measures that people can take to better their chances of a long, healthy life:

- Getting a good education
- Maintaining a sense of control in one's life
- Reducing stress and anxiety
- Regular exercise
- Social interaction and support
- Activities that stimulate the brain

Cohen, in *The Mature Mind*, encourages a "social portfolio" in which he gives older adults guidelines for engaging in both solitary and low-energy group activities, as well as high-energy and mobility group activities, for a socially well-rounded and active older adult. This formula can apply to adults at any age, but in aging adults, keeping up social connections is a high priority. Cohen correlates social engagement with good mental health and withdrawal and social isolation with depression or some other ill.

DESIRE TO SERVE

In addition to changes in the brain and the need to make a concerted effort to stay active and social in later life, there are many truly nice things about growing older that people are generally concerned with, such as relationships with grandchildren, how to use free time through hobbies or new studies, and, particularly with the baby boomer generation, a desire and ability to volunteer and continue to feel viable and useful throughout the aging process.

> Baby Boomers—the generation of 77 million Americans born between 1946 and 1964—represent a potential boon to the volunteer world. Based on U.S. Census data, the numbers of volunteers age 65 and older will increase 50 percent over the next 13 years, from just under 9 million in 2007 to more than 13 million in 2020. What's more, that number will continue to rise for many years to come, as the youngest Baby Boomers will not reach age 65 until 2029. (Foster-Bey, Grimm, and Dietz, 2007)

Not only can libraries serve as a resource for finding good volunteer opportunities within the community, but libraries also *afford* one of the best and most meaningful volunteering opportunities around. According to Williamson, Bannister, and Sullivan (2010) in an article for the September 2010 *Journal of Librarianship and Information Science*, baby boomers will be looking for a different type of volunteering experience, one that meets their needs of flexibility, makes use of their own experience and skills, and offers them something in return—the ability to stay active and involved and to make a difference in their community. For this reason, it seems that baby boomers would make good candidates for assisting with programming in libraries as opposed to sitting at a desk or helping out in tech services unless those tasks should happen to be their areas of expertise.

Numerous studies have indicated that those who volunteer, regardless of their age group, benefit from the experience, and older adults or the newly retired in particular can benefit from the volunteer experience. In "Focusing on the Health Benefits of Volunteering as a Recruitment Strategy," Judy Looman Swinson (2006) lists numerous studies that describe the health and emotional benefits of volunteerism. While most of these studies focus on the *physical* benefits of volunteerism—greater physical activity, reduced blood pressure, and improved immune system—there was also evidence of improved self-esteem, a reduction of anxiety and depression, and a longer life span.

It is no secret that volunteering brings a strong sense of satisfaction to volunteers and serves a tremendous purpose for the agencies for which they volunteer. No wonder volunteering among older adults is increasing, which is one of many reasons why libraries need to capture the attention, influence, and volunteer potential of the older generations.

WHY IS IT SMART FOR LIBRARIANS TO TURN THEIR ATTENTION TO THIS AGE GROUP?

Libraries and older adults are a natural fit, and librarians can play an important role in promoting the well-being of their senior patrons through educational programming. The library becomes a place where seniors can connect and grow, learn new skills and continue to play a vital role in their communities through volunteerism, and engage in active support for the library and its programs. So, as if you needed it, here are just a few simple statements about why librarians should make an effort to engage older adults within their communities:

- Older adults are natural library users. They grew up with libraries. They have childhood memories of the library and are accustomed to receiving information through a visit to the library as opposed to the younger generations, which like to receive information, entertainment, and everything else delivered to a personal portable device.
- Seniors are retired and actually have time to spend at the library.
- The economic downturn has generated a greater need for services, volunteer opportunities, and job-skills development in this age group.
- Older adults are *voters*, and libraries need voters on their side.
- They have volunteer time and a lifetime of skills to offer.
- And, last but not least, they have networks built up over a lifetime of living and can be a great asset in getting out the vote, supporting your mission and goals, and giving freely of their time.

CHAPTER 2

Starting Something Special

No single set-in-stone way exists to create a department for older adults that will fit the needs of *every* community, but there is a way to create a terrific department that will be successful in *your* community. The key is assessment scanning, which allows you to take into account the very aspects that make your community unique and use them to your advantage. To start something special (and successful), your biggest task is to find out more about your community, both in your library and the service community. Creating customized programming is not only just a good practice but is absolutely essential to finding success within your community. First, we will talk about information that you are going to need, and then we will go into detail about the best ways to obtain and analyze that information.

ENVIRONMENTAL ASSESSMENT SCANNING

Assessment scanning is the key to finding out more about what is going on right now in your library and in your community. Most importantly, it also leads to finding out what people in your community want from your senior department. Always use assessment before creating anything new, from an entire department to individual services to library programming; it is an essential step in the planning process that should never be neglected.

Internal Assessment Scanning

Taking a closer look at a variety of facets in your current organization can lead to some wonderful insights. Start by examining your library's history, both politically and culturally, including past and current service priorities. Are they conducive to creating an inviting environment for older adults? Has your library always focused on children? Are you known as a cultural center? Is your library controversial? Is the current culture of the library going to be a road block to the success of your new programs? What can be done to change things?

Next up are the current collateral assets of your library. This is everything from funding to current technology to partnerships that are already in place. Can anything be shuffled around to meet the needs of older adults more successfully? Will you need to focus on funding the program yourself? Are there any beneficial partnerships already in place?

On a daily basis, the library is collecting a wealth of quantitative data on users: number of patrons, computer users, and program attendees as well as circulation statistics. These can function as important baselines for your future evaluation strategies while also giving you current numbers and expectations with which to work.

Next, take a look at your library's current programming and services, especially those that are highly successful or that already seem to draw an older demographic. This is a great way to start making a concrete list of programs and services that can be considered customized and geared toward older adults. This scan is a gold mine because it reveals previously proven programs filled with resources that have already been gathered for past presentations, often including guest speakers and community partners.

Next, it's time to garner what the current staff of the library has to offer. Determine what not only staff, but also volunteers and frequent patrons, suggest; they are a wealth of free resources for programming. This treasure trove of human resources might include world travelers, cultural representatives, experts in various fields, hobbyists, book reviewers, tech geeks, and chefs, all with connections and ideas to share with you. They may be able to provide you with consultation in their area of expertise or be perfectly willing to be a part of the creation and presentation process.

Last but not least, take a detailed look at the current seniors who already use the library. Find out how aware they are of current services, what they like or dislike, and what they would like to see more of in the library. It might be difficult to implement a survey for seniors only, as you don't want to make any assumptions about a person's age; however, in doing any type of survey, ask for demographic information such as age and gender, and distribute the evaluation at events where senior library users are present.

External Scanning

External environmental scans include everything and anything that can be derived from the service community. The foundation of an external scan starts with government census statistics on demographics. Try using American FactFinder online from the U.S. Census Bureau to find age demographics for your area. Take a look at the older adult population and its growth rate, economic status, and language spoken at home. This is valuable information but must be taken in the context of the community at large. Examine your local environment, culture, and politics in detail. This type of information can be garnered from observation and researching local news sources. For example: Does winter affect the use of the library? Do the current Senate members seem to support funding for libraries? What is the housing situation like for seniors in your community? Are there senior living facilities nearby, or plans for new senior housing? What about public transportation convenient to the library, such as a bus stop or even transportation provided exclusively for the elderly or physically disabled? Are there any changes being enacted by the local city government that could affect seniors' ability to use the library, either positively or negatively?

Don't forget community resources such as potential partnerships, free resources for patrons, upcoming events, and anything that could derail possible patron use for the library, such as bus line closures. This will help you plan events with the best (and free) partnerships and help you avoid events on days when other community events will be more popular. This is the time to touch base with local senior centers. They are a great partner to get on board from the very beginning for a number of reasons. First, they have a natural built-in audience that is already accustomed to being out in the community and attending senior-specific programming. Finding out more about the services and programming they offer will allow you to work together to make better programs and services: you can fill in gaps they have, you won't overlap topics, and you can coordinate to create even better events.

INFORMATION-GATHERING TECHNIQUES

Creating a strategy that combines methods is more effective at garnering information from all the various aspects of your community. That way, you can effectively cover all your bases and find your blind spots. The following details a variety of methods for pulling together this assessment information.

Advisory Council

This group should be comprised of community gatekeepers, community partners, patrons, and library staff members. They should meet on a regular basis to discuss action items and offer feedback as well as recommendations. As members of a community dedicated to serving seniors, they have expert knowledge and experience. This is also a great space for them to network and collaborate with each other as well.

Focus Groups

Set up a focus group and invite seniors, both library users and nonusers, to engage in some well-planned Q&A about library services. In *The Accidental Library Marketer*, Kathy Dempsey (2009) suggests that you start by holding a focus group with friendly people, like patrons who already support the library, in order to build your confidence. She suggests that you use humor to put people at ease and let them know that you are really going to thoughtfully consider what they have to say during the course of the discussion and then follow through and make known any changes you are making in the library as a result of their contributions.

Topics for focus groups should only include items upon which the librarians are willing and able to take action. Don't hold a "pie in the sky" focus group about setting up a brand-new senior space in your library when you are already overcrowded or make it seem like you are offering promises you can't keep. The purpose of this type of discussion is to listen and learn in a group interview setting. Include participants from different socioeconomic backgrounds and age groups, from newly retired baby boomers to the elderly. Focus groups can provide more in-depth information than a one- or two-page survey questionnaire, and inviting people into the library to offer their input is an opportunity to start new relationships with this particular demographic.

If you have difficulty interpreting what you have learned from your focus groups, find assistance from a marketing class from a local institution of secondary or higher education. They can also be of assistance with planning, implementing, and analyzing the information you have collected, if you aren't comfortable doing it on your own. College campuses frequently offer this type of opportunity to their marketing students, and this can produce tremendous results at little or no cost. The important thing is to come up with information that is completely unbiased and representative of the user group and then take what you've learned and act on it.

Community Open Houses, Public Forums, and Discussion Groups

Much like focus groups, these community events allow for those who are interested to have their say. They do tend to focus on those who are already interested, as in current user groups, which is, unfortunately, a drawback. However, they also allow the community at large, including those of all ages, to give their opinions on your planning process and can have much to do with the outcomes. Such groups could include community gatekeepers and political leaders.

Personal Interviews

Also much like a focus group, this type of interview allows for a great depth of information to be gathered. For example, you might find nonusers and choose the personal interview route to find out more about them and their reasons for never visiting the library. Personal interviews with community gatekeepers will transform your once informal conversation into a data-mining process that can be better used for presentation to the library board. Personal interviews can be conducted with current users as well.

Observation

What is going on at your library on any given day? Have staff take a guesstimate survey of users entering the facility by age. What else did they notice? Are the older patrons having trouble finding resources? Do they make a beeline toward the computers? Just the observation of day-to-day occurrences can lend some valuable insights.

Surveys

These simple little questionnaires are easy to create and analyze, and, best of all, they contain information that is vital to planning. They can be given to current users, nonusers, and community partners. Multiple routes are available for getting the surveys to these groups, including via an online survey linked from the library website, Facebook page, and any Twitter accounts. It can be sent out in a mass email to cardholders. It can be passed out in person as a flier in any outgoing library correspondence, including checkout receipts to patrons in the library and surrounding community and as outreach to community partners and gatekeepers. The types of questions used in a survey can range from simple yes or no questions to scales, ranked items, "check all that apply," and finally to qualitative open-ended questions. The following sample surveys are included in Appendix B: Assessment Survey for Older Adults: Current Users; Assessment Survey for Older Adults: Current Nonusers; Assessment Survey for Community Gatekeepers; and Assessment Survey for Library Staff.

ASSESSING YOUR INFORMATION— PUTTING IT ALL TOGETHER

Once all your information is gathered, it's time to put it all together. For quantitative data, you can use an online survey tool of your choice. See Appendix C for recommend free technology tools. Look under the "Assessment/Evaluation" header.

For qualitative data, the common threads need to be found. Start by underlining key words, phrases, and anything that stands out. These threads will function as data points. Count up each keyword and theme, grouping them accordingly, and start by looking for patterns. For example, responses such as "lack of lighting," "too dark," "hard to see what I am reading," and "dim" could all be grouped under the overall thread of "improper lighting." Once your data has been analyzed, some easy-to-fix problems may jump out, while other issues are more complex and may warrant a focus group. For example, if many patrons suggested they just don't hear about library programs or events, it's time to learn about the media outlets from which they get their information. This point could then be included in an upcoming survey or focus group.

Sharing Your Findings

Make sure to bring together your results in a presentation-style format that is easily understandable by persons of interest outside the library, such as stakeholders and future funders. Present your findings to them professionally, in the same manner in which you would present to colleagues or board members. Include a cover sheet with a summary of important findings and recommendations, a title page, a table of contents, a statement of purpose with background information, your methodology, your findings shown as charts and graphs, a discussion of the results, recommendations, a conclusion, and an appendix with a source list and copies of blank survey forms.

FUNDING: LOOKING FOR ASSISTANCE—INSIDE AND OUT

The results of your assessment, namely the recommendations, are a valuable asset for attempting to get funding, but sometimes there just isn't any money, period. That's when it's time either to do your own form of fundraising through grants and creative fund-raising events or look for free or donated resources.

In-House Resources

The current library staff is one of your most important financial resources. Their job is to make the library better, and they are already being paid. So break up their monotony and consult with them or steal them away for an hour to plan and present to seniors.

Often, public librarians have specialized knowledge. They work in one department and have an extensive set of knowledge in that one area. So if you are in a larger library and starting a new program for older adults, it is time for you to break out of your own rut and take advantage of those who are in a different rut, so to speak. For example, perhaps your library has a well-rounded collection of materials on local history. In fact, when a local historical society closed a few years ago, all their materials were sent to the library, but only the librarian in the history section really cared about it. Time to find out more and make a new program!

Remember those staff surveys? Perhaps the children's librarian knows how to teach knitting and is willing to present. What about the person shelving books from the browsing library? He reports that he set up a Nintendo Wii system at his aunt's senior center and can recommend games..

If you are in a small library and your staff is limited, ask them about people they know in the community who might be willing to help with programming. You may think you know everyone and what they could offer; however, someone may suggest something a neighbor or relative could provide.

Technology can be a big issue in a library, and every specialized department would prefer a custom setup. (The wish list for a senior department could go on and on: a bay of computers, a set of digital cameras and camcorders, and a gaming platform or two, with plenty of controllers, perhaps an audio system, and maybe some GPS units to borrow.) While this may not be possible yet, by keeping up-to-date on the current schedule for the computer lab, multimedia resources, and even teens' video game platforms you can make your senior department or program technology rich. It is simply a matter of getting creative on the timing and planning well in advance. Your patrons and community may not realize how much your seniors need and want these items, so be sure to make it known publicly how much donations would be appreciated, and you should always be on the lookout for grant opportunities.

External Resources

Locating speakers who are willing to share what they know at no cost or, at the very least, for a token of appreciation are often easy to find. Local community members love to find an opportunity to showcase their skills, improve their community, and provide themselves with a marketing plug, especially those baby boomers who want to keep their skills honed and stay active. Contact your local celebrities, artists, professors, and health experts to spend an hour or so promoting their talent or service, and do yourself, your patrons, and the local talent a favor by allowing them to showcase their skills and knowledge while filling a patron and library need. We all know that local government agencies, such as the city or county department of health or social services, are always willing to send speakers at no cost to represent community services. It's just a matter of finding willing partners, establishing great working relationships, and keeping your contact information current.

Local businesses often love an opportunity to donate—just make sure they have that opportunity. Marketing to older adults allows businesses to access a market that is loyal and often prolific in their patronization. So drum up some potentials; it can't hurt to send a request. A donation of a box or two of donuts for every program may be just the thing you need to increase your program morale. Work with your staff to start to identify local clubs and/or organizations that provide donations, like the local Elks Lodge or a locally owned business.

If you have a local events planner, he or she may be willing to give you contact lists, send a representative to provide a preview of an upcoming event, or even bring along a guest presenter from the actual event. For example, if there is a genealogy convention in the area, a marketing rep might be willing to come by and talk about the event in your events prep (see chapter 4) series and bring some samples, maps for parking, and discount coupons.

If you are determined to spend some of that budget money, just remember: keep it thrifty when launching a new program or project. Partner with other local libraries or branches to share costs on guest speakers. Use those local sponsors. Regular contact with the community at large can help promote the library as a free venue for events that an outside source might pay for, or, failing free, you might be able to negotiate a smaller fee for a performer or author already booked to do another gig in your area.

GRANTING YOUR WISHES

Exploring grant opportunities is a must in the current economy. Local or state art council grants can be used to develop art exhibits or pay for performers. Technology grants, possibly available through LSTA funding from your state library, can bolster the number of public service computers or even create a traveling computer lab to take to local senior centers. Assistive technology loan programs are available in most states. Borrowing a particular item will allow you to try out a screen reader or magnifier prior to making an expensive purchase, and technology grants can frequently be used for assistive technology as well as standard computer technology. Sign up for every list you can find for grants, and partner with other librarians in your surrounding area or in branch libraries to win large-scale programming grants. On a local level, you should always look at grants offered by your own state, such as an arts council, department of education, or humanities council, as well as foundations and corporations that have "giving" programs. The following suggested grants could be applied to a variety of program types. For more ideas as to their potential applications, see the wide variety of programming suggestions in chapter 4.

Grant Search Websites

The Programming Librarian website, funded by a grant from the Institute of Museum and Library Services (IMLS) to the American Library Association Public Programs Office to assist librarians in finding authoritative resources for cultural programming, lists programming grants. They are constantly changing and updating, so keep a close eye on this one. See which grants work best for your library, and enlist a coconspirator to help plan a dual-department program. Keep an eye out for a library-wide grant with a particular benefit for your seniors, bring it up at staff meetings, and better yet . . . spearhead it!

Website: http://www.programminglibrarian.org/library-grants.html

The Foundation Center offers a searchable website, updated weekly, and provides the most comprehensive and accurate information on U.S. grant makers and their funding activities. Find out if your state publishes a foundation directory for a listing of state-level grant opportunities, and don't forget that many state libraries offer competitive grants to libraries, as well as humanities and arts councils. There's funding out there, you just have to be willing to go after it.

Website: http://foundationcenter.org

Government Grants

- Administration on Aging
  Website: http://www.aoa.gov/AoARoot/Grants/index.aspx
- Grants.gov (lists all federal grants)
  Website: http://www.grants.gov

- Institute of Museum and Library Services
  Website: http://www.imls.gov/applicants/applicants.shtm
- National Endowment for the Arts
  Website: http://www.nea.gov/grants/index.html
- National Endowment for the Humanities (NEH)
  Website: http://www.neh.gov/grants/index.html
  They offer the Picturing America Grant, which gives funding to humanities-based programs in public libraries that highlight the NEH's Picturing America artwork collection. This grant could be solicited for a potential art series in conjunction with a learning local series.
  Website: http://picturingamerica.neh.gov
- National Library of Medicine
  Website: http://www.nlm.nih.gov/grants.html

Other Grants

- AARP Foundation
  Website: http://www.aarp.org/aarp-foundation/Grants-Administration/
  AARP provides lots of news about their own grants and partner grants; however, information is not organized into one category.
- AstraZeneca Pharmaceuticals
  Website: http://www.astrazeneca-us.com/community-support
- Atlantic Philanthropies
  Website: http://www.atlanticphilanthropies.org/search/grants
  This company supplies a searchable database of grants.
- Cooperative Development Foundation
  Website: http://www.cdf.coop/applying-and-reporting
  This foundation accepts grants that exhibit "cooperative solutions for seniors in rural communities in the U.S." Also, there is a yearly subtheme, which is for a narrower aspect of their overarching topic.
- Harry and Jeanette Weinberg Foundation
  Website: http://hjweinbergfoundation.org/grants/
  The foundation provides grants in many applicable areas.
- Humana
  Website: http://www.humana.com/resources/about/corporate/hcb
- MetLife Foundation
  Website: http://bit.ly/uLnKK
- The Grantsmanship Center
  Website: http://www.tgci.com/funding.shtml
- Pepsi Refresh Project
  Website: http://www.refresheverything.com
  This project allows anyone to submit his or her idea, and then the website viewers vote for their favorite. This program would be great for the Urban Garden program, the Story Bee program, or almost anything in the Tech Bytes technology series, but you will, of course, have ideas of your own. See chapter 4 for these programs and many others.
- Robert Wood Johnson Foundation
  Website: http://www.rwjf.org/grants
  Offers grants for programs that must improve health or health care.
- Verizon Grant
  Website: http://foundation.verizon.com/grant/guidelines.shtml

This organization offers financial assistance for the following categories: education, literacy, health care and accessibility, and Internet safety. The Wellness Watch series, Tech Bytes series, and the Story Bee program (see chapter 4) can all benefit from these grants.

- WellPoint
Website: http://www.wellpointfoundation.org/
They offer grants related to public-health related issues. The Wellness Watch series is a good candidate for seeking out this type of grant (see chapter 4).

MAKING A SENIOR PROGRAM A WINNING PROPOSITION

Now that you have a boatload of information from your assessment as well as some funding plans, it's time to turn your attention toward getting the senior program off the ground. You might encounter some difficulty in persuading your staff or board that a senior-specific program is right for your library. After all, who has room for one more "special" space or collection, and how can staff continue to expand their range of duties in the workplace? In the same manner that you will later market your programs and services to seniors, you may have to market the same idea to your staff and board. Of course, having the board's approval might make selling your staff on the idea just a bit easier. In selling your new idea, it is important to do the following:

- Know your board and its decision-making history.
- Professionally present the information from your assessment scan.
- Focus on the possibilities: grants, partnerships, and already obtained resources.
- Propose the idea: space, programming, and services. (You may have to skip ahead in this book to get those ideas rolling.)
- Sell the ease of implementation: give all the reasons why the whole process would be easy, smooth, inexpensive, and more than worthwhile.
- Make use of everything at your disposal to create an effective presentation for your board. Perhaps something like the presentation of video interviews with local seniors who support your project could be included as part of your presentation.

CARVE OUT A SPACE

Now that you have the approval, it's time to get started. You might have the luxury of creating an actual space for older patrons. If that's the case, these next few sections will provide you with the ideas and know-how.

The downtown Salt Lake City Public Library has an entire (and amazing) floor dedicated to children and half a floor just for teens. This library was built new and customized but does not have a place for seniors. While not every single demographic needs their own space in every library, there are many compelling reasons to create a senior space, and it has been done quite successfully at quite a few libraries.

In 2007, Assistant Director Allan Kleiman of the Old Bridge Public Library in Old Bridge, New Jersey, launched a new senior space with funding from the INFOLINK Regional Cooperative, the New Jersey State Library, and Old Bridge Public Library. Kleiman, a long-time library veteran with extensive experience in creating programs for older adults, was able to create his dream space for serving these loyal library users, complete with programming, meeting, and learning space. The library followed a bookstore model so patrons could more easily browse materials. Many senior-friendly elements were used, such as closed-circuit televisions, audiobooks, large-print materials, and oversized computer monitors. A comfortable "living room" was set up for sitting and reading a book or the newspaper, a "memory space" offers a flat display case for creating exhibits with memorabilia, and the "front porch" offers wooden rocking chairs to sit and knit, share a story, or talk with your neighbor.

Carving out a space was just the beginning. Kleiman went on to engage his senior library users in video gaming, social networking online, creating their own blog, and he provided extensive programs for his seniors. He was one of the first librarians to introduce seniors to the joys and benefits of Wii gaming, and many librarians followed suit with the idea of gaming for older adults. Kleiman has shared his message of creating a space for seniors with libraries around the world through presentations and writings and continues his work through consulting in the design of several adult spaces in Pennsylvania and New Jersey libraries. The Old Bridge senior space is considered a prototype for libraries everywhere (McDonald, 2011).

AND WHY SHOULD WE DO THIS?

So, really, why do seniors need a space all their own? In addition to all the previous reasons, studies show that multitasking is not ideal for older adults. If multitasking is the new normal for the millennial generation, *focusing* is the norm for most older adults. Numerous studies suggest that it has to do with an aging brain, and of course it does, but we would also like to suggest that it has something to do with a lifetime habit of focusing on one task at a time. Applying oneself to a single purpose at a time brings more satisfaction to those who grew up only reading or only working on a single project, at the most listening to background music at the same time. Providing a relatively quiet place for older adults to read or have book discussions is a small service that most libraries can provide. Sometimes the only way to accomplish something is to just make it happen. So get creative, get innovative, and get started. Carve out a space and a place for seniors at your library by giving it a little thought and elbow grease.

Location, Location, Location

If you're really short on space, just pick a secluded corner not too far from the front door and restrooms, but out of the line of sight of the main thoroughfare and the noisy, hectic children's section, as your small senior space. Each library is different, and sometimes the only way to create such a space will be to pick a spot and use existing furniture and shelving to create a cozy nook. How difficult can that be? And think of the rewards, the pleasure and honor you will bring to your seniors by making this simple gesture. Do you *have to* have a space just for seniors? Not necessarily. Services and programming are more important, but setting a goal to create such a space is also worthwhile, even if it's just a goal for the future.

Space Dynamics

When designing your space, consider the concept of universal design, or designing for an environment that is usable by the most people to the greatest extent possible, including those with or without disabilities or special needs. Designing a space that can serve all of the people, all of the time, is just smart design, and even entire cities are getting in on universal design, or at least thinking about it. A recent *USA Today* (2011) newspaper article, "Aging Boomers Strain Cities Built for the Young," clearly demonstrates that city planners are now realizing they have a big problem in cities designed for the fleet of foot as they are faced with an ever-aging population now dwelling in these poorly designed cities. If entire cities are dealing with this issue now, it is surely time for libraries to do the same. Consider the following characteristics when creating your space.

Furniture and Shelving

Ideally, the furniture is comfortable but easy enough to rise from. This will help counter any problems with balance or hip/joint issues that some seniors experience. Computer seating should not be on wheels, which will prevent sliding while moving to a standing position. A variety of stable stools can be provided in the shelving aisles in case a patron browses to the point of needing a seat or somewhere to set books that are too heavy to carry. Kiosks, computer stations, and shelving can all be set up to encourage the feeling of a separate space while still providing access that complies with American Disability Association guidelines. Should tall standard shelving be used? Base this on your patron surveys. Bending and reaching can be problematic, but you may find that your patron base is relatively fit and healthy, in which case standard shelving is a good fit. If you only have space for a few shelves, use the lower to middle shelves, eliminating the very lowest and highest shelves. You can always use the top shelves for display and to promote upcoming speakers and programming.

Kiosks

Having a dedicated kiosk or display case for your space will add to its legitimacy within the library. Include general subject area book displays or books related to upcoming workshops or programs. A display case allows for items of interest to be displayed from the library's collections or from collections outside the library. If using collections from other agencies for display, consider entering into a borrower's agreement with the lending agency. Most lending agencies will have an agreement already in place. For your own sake, just be sure to have documentation of the transaction, including photographs of the items as they are taken into your custody. You don't want to be held liable for damage that occurred in transit or that was in place before you received the objects.

Space for Childhood Favorites

Within your senior space, you might want to create a shelf of classic children's books, which seniors could check out to read to their grandchildren. A few titles to add to this shelf could be the following:

Complete Tales of Winnie-the-Pooh by A. A. Milne
Pippi Longstocking by Astrid Lindgren
Mary Poppins by P. L. Travers
The Incredible Journey by Sheila Burnford
Charlotte's Web by E. B. White
Babe: The Gallant Pig by Dick King-Smith
Where the Wild Things Are by Maurice Sendak
Complete Tales: The 23 Original Peter Rabbit Books by Beatrix Potter
Mike Mulligan and His Steam Shovel by Virginia Lee Burton

Of course, any Dr. Seuss books would be a good addition to this shelf, but you get the idea. Having a shelf of children's books on hand could encourage some quality reading time with grandma or grandpa.

Outdoor Spaces

Setting aside a private outside space is a great way to allow for quiet reading and communion with nature. If there is any interest, the outdoor space could include a small garden, raised vegetable beds, or a flower bed, such as a rose garden. Even if you aren't in a warm climate, an outdoor space for your library is still a good idea and can be used several months of the year. Intergenerational programming is a good fit for learning about gardening and nature. We like the name Solar Senior Arboretum. Get creative; tear up some of that high-maintenance lawn and make a wonderful garden and reading area where older adults can enjoy spending their time.

BRANDING YOUR PROGRAM

Picking out a name for your overall program, and even for the space you set aside for the senior area, makes everything more noticeable and memorable, not to mention being a great jumping-off point for an entire branding scheme. We like to refer to it as "naming the puppy." Just like naming a puppy, it makes it harder to give up a program if it has an official name. Keep in mind the feeling you want your program to have when making this decision. Pay attention to the fine line between being trivial or cutesy and being flat-out boring and unmemorable. Also, keep in mind the risks of using the words like *senior* or *elderly*. You may scare off or even offend the right age patrons who don't consider themselves old or senior or especially elderly. These potential patrons would still love to have programs and a space set aside for them but won't sign on for categorizing themselves as old. It's not just denial, since seniors today are more active and healthy than ever, and they don't feel old or want to be thought of as old. Knowing your community can help you find the branding style that suits your patrons best. If you'd rather not take on this task yourself, hold a contest for choosing the name of the new program. Don't be afraid to use a name already in use (but be sure to ask permission), and have some fun!

List Names of Programs Already in Use

Silver Surfers (see Joseph, 2006)
Connections Café (Tempe Public Library, Arizona)
Senior Space—Old Bridge Public Library (Old Bridge, New Jersey)

Other Ideas

Solar Seniors
Empty Nesters and Soaring Seniors
Finding Your Wings Project
Blazing New Paths
New Paths from Old
The Second Act
The Second Chapter
Chapter II
Second Chance Seekers
The Late Bloomers Club
Growth in Aging Project
Phase II Project

DEFINING THE IDEAL—WORKING WITH THE REALITIES

It's easy to imagine the ideal and most wonderful space. Say, for example, a whole level of your library set aside just for seniors with a nice entryway filled with art objects or even posters and with a dedicated librarian or volunteer patiently waiting to answer questions, to give tours, promote services, and to research and plan programming. Let's not forget a specialized bay of computer stations, an assortment of e-readers, a Nintendo Wii or two, a presentation area, perhaps a meeting room, amazingly comfortable seating, a wide selection of books and magazines, tasteful décor, and topped off with a brilliant marketing campaign.

Easier said than done? Think again! Always start with the ideals: what would a much-beloved and used space look like at your library? It's that very vision that will help lay a foundation for gradual realization. It provides a basis for creating both realistic and practical long- and short-term goals. Keeping that ultimate vision in mind allows upcoming opportunities and ideas to revolve around and be incorporated into the larger picture, removing the limitations of a smaller, albeit realistic vision.

CHAPTER 3

Stellar Services

Services are those little touches that make a library department really stand apart, stand out, and shine. The following is our dream list of those extras from which you can pick and choose for your own custom services offerings.

SPECIAL SENIOR SERVICES DESK

Like a concierge desk, seniors using the special senior services desk will have access to more than just reference help. Given the staffing availability, a concierge service philosophy is what is called for in serving this deserving portion of the population. This personal attention and attention to detail is priceless and will be greatly appreciated, particularly when it comes to using new technologies that might create a challenge for some older adults. Through this desk, they could have the ability to do the following:

1. Reserve attendance and/or special seating for events, such as seats near an exit or an aisle seat. Some older adults might have had to make a huge effort to get to an event and can't readily scoot into a mid-row seat. Consider, too, that some events might be prohibitive to seniors if they are held mostly at night or if seating is first come first serve, and consider that there may be other complications that should be taken into account, like challenges with hearing or a need for restroom access.
2. Receive senior citizen discount prices for nonlibrary events hosted on the library grounds.
3. Receive free parking vouchers.
4. Arrange escorts for assisting senior patrons to and from parking garages and nearby public transportation.
5. Arrange for mobile book service and postage-paid book services.
6. Sign up for all library programming and classes.

7. Receive social service referral.
8. Ask for assistance with resource navigation.

While such a customized service may be out of reach for many libraries, perhaps offering a concierge desk service one or two afternoons a week, using volunteers or part-time staff, would be more realistic. Making the library welcoming and, most importantly, accessible to seniors or other individuals with any level of disability is the right thing to do.

SENIORS WEBPAGE

Many libraries now have a webpage for seniors as part of their website offering. We think that an entire website for seniors works best. There is simply too much to include and interact with for a single webpage to work in this instance. Some items we suggest for inclusion on the site are the following:

- Book reviews by patrons
- Tutorials
- Upcoming events
- Links to in-house and out-of-house resources
- Blog of past events
- Announcements of current events

This site should be custom created, easy to update by senior department staff, and, ideally, updated on a daily basis. Where feasible, a senior department staff website can be created and the library website homepage can feature a link to this new site. Ample free software is available online for website creation. One easy-to-use website creator is Webs (http://www.webs.com). It features templates, tutorials, and easy-to-update webpages. Sites created with this software, because they are free, come with ads across the top of the page, but for a small monthly fee those banners can be removed. (Last price check was as low as $3.75 a month, a thrifty price for easily updatable customization.)

In "Making Your Web Site Senior Friendly," the National Institute on Aging and the National Network of Libraries of Medicine created a checklist for those wishing to design websites for older adults or adults with low vision. They suggest, at a minimum, to make the following accommodations:

- Use a sans serif typeface, such as Helvetica, that is not condensed. Avoid the use of serif, novelty, and display typefaces.
- Use 12-point or 14-point type size for body text.
- Use medium or bold-face type.
- Present body text in upper and lowercase letters. Use all capital letters and italics in headlines only. Reserve underlining for links.
- Double-space all body text.
- Of the three ways to justify type—left, full, or center justified—left-justified text is optimal for older adults.
- Avoid yellow and blue and green in close proximity. These colors and juxtapositions are difficult for some older adults to discriminate. Ensure that text and graphics are understandable when viewed on a black-and-white monitor.
- Use dark type or graphics against a light background, or white lettering on a black or dark-colored background. Avoid patterned backgrounds.
- Present information in a clear and familiar way to reduce the number of inferences that must be made. Use positive statements.

- Write the text in simple language. Provide an online glossary of technical terms.
- Organize the content in a standard format. Break lengthy documents into short sections.
- Use text-relevant images only.
- Provide text alternatives such as open-captioning or access to a static version of the text for all animation, video, and audio.

Many other suggestions for making a website senior friendly, including suggestions for layout and design, are available at http://www.nlm.nih.gov/pubs/checklist.pdf.

E-READERS

E-readers are a wonderful option for older adults as they easily make text larger, brighter, or darker, thereby increasing legibility. E-readers are lightweight and can store many books on a single device, reducing the weight a patron has to carry. While many librarians have yet to jump into the e-book arena, and particularly the area of lending e-readers as there are serious questions about the legitimacy of loaning some reading devices, some e-reader producers are making library loaning simple and easy. Barnes and Noble, for example, has openly engaged libraries in the loan of its Nook e-reader. In October 2010, Lisa Rossi reported in *ColumbiaPatch* about a partnership between Howard County (Maryland) Library and a local Barnes and Noble to train patrons in the use of 60 new Nooks purchased by the library. The Howard County Library announced the partnership and began to loan 60 Nook e-readers in December. At the time, it was a pilot program designed to teach people how to use the device and gave library cardholders access to popular titles in the electronic format. Nooks e-readers were preloaded with 34 titles chosen from bestsellers and book club favorites (Rossi, 2010). Even Amazon has recently announced the sanction of the use of its e-reader, complete with note-taking facility, for e-book library loans. This trend is only going to continue as producers of e-readers realize that libraries are major players in the e-book and e-reader arena.

If the future of libraries and the e-book phenomena remains a mystery that only time will unravel, the constant evolution of these devices is an even greater mystery; however, we can be certain that the e-reader will continue to change. If the rate of change in current technology is any indication, the changes should be rapid and many. Predictions of interactive, multimedia, collaborative, and virtual experience electronic books are everywhere, and such products are already in use on a smaller scale.

While e-books and e-readers will continue to change, we can also be certain that libraries have to be a part of the e-book/e-reader revolution and that our older adults, like the rest of our patrons, should not be left out of this exciting period in the evolution of the book. If you are embarking upon a program to purchase and circulate e-readers in your library, make sure that your seniors know about the service and give them the opportunity to learn about the devices and use them just like your teens and younger adults. They are amazing devices, and being a certain age does not automatically preclude interest in new technologies, especially ones with such great potential benefits for the older user.

COMPUTER/BOOK ENHANCEMENT PROGRAMS

Readability

Readability is a free computer program that can easily be downloaded (at http://lab.arc90.com/experiments/readability) on a single computer designated for seniors or a whole bank of them if you have a larger senior space. When activated while viewing a webpage, Readability allows seniors to see a decluttered version of the article they are viewing. It removes all the ads and confusing Flash, leaving just the text of the article. The patron can then choose to resize the Web article for better viewing. It is a great program for providing clarity and ease of use for overpopulated websites, of which there are many. Patrons can also easily install this program on their home computers.

Zoom Text

Zoom Text allows patrons to easily enlarge any part of the computer screen. Zoom Text is software for purchase; however, you can sign up for a free trial at http://www.aisquared.com/zoomtext.

JAWS Screen Accessibility Software

The JAWS software program reads aloud what is on the computer screen. JAWS is a bit pricy, but again, there is a free demo online (at http://www.freedomscientific.com/products/fs/jaws-product-page.asp), which can help you decide if this product is right for your library. JAWS also offers Braille output, converting the text on the computer screen to printed Braille.

Braille Displays and Printers

[Braille displays] operate by raising and lowering different combinations of pins electronically to produce in Braille what appears on a portion of the computer screen. They show up to 80 characters from the screen and are refreshable, that is, they change continuously as the user moves around on the screen. The Braille display sits on the user's desk, often underneath the computer keyboard. The advantage of the Braille display in comparison to synthetic speech is in its direct access to information, the ability to check format, spacing and spelling, and the fact that it is quiet. (American Foundation for the Blind, 2011)

Braille printers can actually emboss Braille onto paper. The Braille counterparts to ink printers, they use solenoids to control embossing pins and typically print on heavyweight paper. They are much slower and noisier than regular printers or Braille displays.

THE FUTURE OF COMPUTING: GESTURE-BASED COMPUTING

Much like the Microsoft Kinect system for entertainment and gaming, computers will soon be able to interact with people on a whole new level. According to the *Horizon Report* (New Media Consortium, 2011), there are many upcoming developments that will allow users to interact with a computer through gestures. Gesture-based computing would allow those who have use of their arms freedom from the confines of a keyboard and mouse for many tasks, which could prove beneficial to older adults suffering from arthritis of the hands and fingers. While still in the future, gesture-based computing could make computer usage easier for everyone, including seniors.

LITTLE EXTRAS

Many libraries offer free plastic bags; while nice, they are easily broken and hard to carry. Why not go the extra mile and offer older patrons free book bags? These can be obtained cheaply from a number of companies or solicited as donations, and these book bags can be branded with the company who made the donation and your library's logo or even the logo of your senior program. They make for good marketing. The Friends of the Library could donate their old book bags, or bags could be purchased at a dollar store or even at a local thrift store. This sort of attention to detail can go a long way toward making sure older library patrons make it home with their books in tow.

OUTREACH SERVICES

Although outreach services are described by the American Library Association's Office for Literacy and Outreach Services in its mission statement as "services that are inclusive of traditionally underserved populations, including new and non-readers, people geographically isolated, people with disabilities, rural and urban poor people, and people generally discriminated against based on race, ethnicity, sexual orientation, age, language and social class," in many libraries, "outreach services" refers to the services that are taken outside the library by library employees, such as bookmobile, in-home library service, and deposit collections in institutions. Outreach services are better covered in an entire book, but here, outreach services play an important role in services to older adults with physical disabilities and those in institutional settings.

Many public libraries offer delivery service to older adults living in senior living facilities or nursing homes or mail or delivery service to those of all ages with a disability preventing them from traveling to the library. These types of services, as with any service, vary in size and scope from library to library, depending on the library's overall staffing, budget, and commitment to such service. While bigger library systems can operate a fleet of bookmobiles and vans, all going to various locations at once, smaller libraries might operate outreach services using volunteers and their personal vehicles. Whatever your case may be, making an effort to extend your library's services to those who cannot come to the library is a worthwhile endeavor.

Some things to consider when thinking of offering a new outreach service:

1. Where can I get the most bang for my buck for outreach to seniors? Is there a local senior center, nursing home, or senior living facility where you could reach a number of older adults at a time?
2. What are my budgetary needs, or am I trying to start a new service without a real budget? It is not advisable to pursue with no budget, but it might be a starting point.
3. If there is no budget, how can I recruit volunteers for outreach services to deliver books to institutions or individuals at home?
4. Consider safety issues and insurance requirements when sending anyone out to act on behalf of the library.
5. Choose your volunteers carefully and have a screening process, job description, and interview before "hiring" them for the job. It is better to be safe than sorry.

EMAIL OR MAILING LIST

Creating an email or regular mailing list is easy to do with just a little time. A simple mailing or email list can grow into a monthly newsletter down the road. You could even have separate email or mailing lists for patrons and community partners. It is imperative to create a network of contacts in the community that extends from the patrons themselves to caregivers and community gatekeepers. Of course, you should ask individuals if they want to be part of a mailing list and get permission from your community contacts as well. Make the list, whether it is by email or regular mail, as personalized as possible in keeping with the concierge theme.

SENIOR ADVISORY BOARD

If you've already begun small and grown your program or are planning to begin a new program, there's no reason you can't round up a few of your best patrons over the age of 65 and create a senior advisory board. This group can be drawn from community gatekeepers, patrons, and Friends of the Library volunteers and can be instrumental in helping you create a program that will be appealing to current library users and attractive to nonusers, as well. Having an advisory board to help with programming ideas and to share the good news of what is happening in your library for seniors can be a big plus.

CONCLUSION

Getting started with a new service for seniors can be as simple as setting up a great newsletter via an email or mailing list or offering a kiosk featuring free handouts on community services for seniors. Whatever stellar services you decide to include at your library, we hope they become an integral and growing part of a larger plan to create a successful department for your senior patron base.

CHAPTER 4

Enterprising Programs

Your senior patrons have been in the world for a spell, and they've seen lots of fads come and go. They want something new and innovative to catch their attention, spur their creativity, and above all be easy to access and participate in, which means that as a librarian, you need to be a cut above creative. Basing your programming on patron needs and wants is an important goal that takes time to evolve. If you're not quite there yet, we have plenty of practical, thrifty, fun, educational, and interesting ideas all planned out for you. All our programs have a few fundamentals in common.

THE FUNDAMENTALS

Umbrella Themes

Often programming for adults can be piecemeal, an idea here and there put onto the calendar. This actually works well for smaller facilities with limited staffing. It is also a great way to start out a new seniors-based program series and determine which events and topics were the most popular. However, given the opportunity, we would like to recommend constructing your yearly programs under the structure of *umbrella themes*. This involves choosing a broad theme, like technology, and planning a year's worth of once-a-month (or more) events based just on that theme. A larger library could have anywhere from 2 to 10 monthly events just for seniors, with each event falling under a different umbrella theme, such as Technology Tuesdays, for example.

Connectivity

How does each program connect older adults to the world around them? As we learned in chapter 1, it is essential to help this population build bridges and stay connected to their communities. Providing ways that they can connect to the library, each other, and the community at large are essential to a successful program. Neglecting the provision of additional resources and outlets in the community on any given topic, during the course of a library program, would be like teaching a class on how to make ice cream without providing the addresses to supply shops, ice cream lover clubs, and ice cream parlors to get ideas for new flavors. Providing these community links is an essential component of connectivity. Technology, of course, adds a wonderful component to this, making connectivity resources easy for you to find and easy for patrons to access.

Patrons can be connected in several ways:

- *To the library*: Patrons can connect through book displays on a program's topic, reading lists, and upcoming related events fliers.
- *To the community*: Community ties can be fostered via handouts with more information on community resources, events, and volunteer opportunities.
- *To other people*: Relationships can be created through a number of routes. One is intergenerational programming, such as bringing in teens and children for shared programming and events. This allows two very different age groups to share in learning and to infuse enthusiasm and fun into any activity. A second way is simply to allow time before and after programs for older adults to get to know each other. A third way is to invite other groups or organizations for shared events—think college student groups and environmental clubs.
- *To the world at large*: Create links through a reference list to worldwide organizations. This can be presented as a list of online links on the senior website or a handout with the links as well as names, phone numbers, and addresses. An example of this would be worldwide volunteering organizations or wildlife conservatories.

Continue the Journey

An hour-long introduction to a topic could be the spark to ignite a flame. How can seniors learn more about the topic? A display table with in-house materials, a link on the website to additional resources, or even a handout with ways to explore further, will all be a welcome addition to your programming. It will also help plant some seeds for future programming on the topic should it be revisited in the next year or two. For example, if there is a program on square dancing, you should provide a handout on community center classes, continuing education classes at the local university, and a list of schools in the area (especially those that offer a senior discount or two!). A book list, even including titles of books the library doesn't have, wouldn't be remiss either. If you mark those currently in print, seniors may choose to buy them, or you can offer to get copies through interlibrary loan.

Learning Goals

Learning goals are simply what should be covered during the course of the program. If you have a broad topic, the learning goals would be the areas that you want to make sure get touched upon during the course of the presentation. This way, you can make sure beforehand that the right speakers and resources are prepped to cover those topics. For example: if the topic is hiking, you could pick and choose from a variety of learning goals to meet your participants' individual needs, including the right gear, local spots, potential dangers, wildlife photography, respecting the environment, dealing with insects, and climates. You might only choose three of these, but if you do, it's important to gear your resources to cover those three completely. See example learning goals in the upcoming sample programs.

Outcomes = Ready-Made Evaluation

We all know the importance of evaluation. By using evaluations, it is a breeze to determine how well a program is working and have the evidence in hand to support its continuation or the evidence to implement change.

Evaluations are much easier to create with the inclusion of outcomes for every program. Outcomes are measurements by which you can determine if your program has made an impact. By ensuring the outcomes match what the program is supposed to accomplish via its learning goals, you allow a clear path for success. Creating an evaluation is then a simple matter of checking whether the program outcomes were met. See chapter 6 for how to create outcomes and evaluate programs using them.

We suggest that you prepare in advance for evaluating your programs. An easy way to start is to always use a sign-up sheet that lists age, even if that seems off-putting to some. This will give you a great data set for what age group is attending and what programs they are coming to. Another necessity is to have surveys prepared in advance. Worst-case scenario, have a generic handout that includes a variety of ways to give feedback, such as a link to the website's feedback box. Additionally, attendance records, connectivity potential, and patron feedback should be included with all evaluations.

Resource and Technology Infusion

Libraries exist to provide access to information, so we believe that everything from the presentation to activities and "continuing the journey" resources should be infused with connections to technology and multiple forms of information. This allows for a variety of learning and interaction styles. Presenting resources in this way is also a means for marketing other programs and services. For example, a presenting author may show you his or her blog, pointing out resources or just photos of his or her journey. This may inspire an attending patron to take the blogging program coming up the following month. It's a great way to introduce small pieces of technology and drum up enthusiasm about them in a subtle, natural way. Remember, older adults, especially baby boomers, want to feel that they are not being left behind, and helping them feel technically connected is an important part of that. We have included a comprehensive list of free Web technology resources in Appendix C for your use.

The bottom line is that resources and access to information are what make the library so special. If a program consists of a just a guest speaker, then a fundamental purpose of the library is being ignored. For every program in this chapter, it was important for us to create ways to infuse our library resources, materials, and technology, as well as our knowledge of outside resources, into the program. Additionally, we have included programs designed to appeal to baby boomers, many of whom have been swept up in the going green movement and have a high level of interest in eco-friendly information. In this chapter, you will find ideas for programs and accompanying resources from which you can pick and choose and, of course, find inspiration for your own programming ideas!

A note on Web addresses provided in this book: We include a number of Web address, full of up-to-date information and well-written articles and videos. We have endeavored to provide you, the reader, with the most accurate and up-to-date website addresses. However, due to the ever-changing and fluid nature of the World Wide Web, these addresses will and do change. Often these changes are minimal—the original website is still there, but the article you are looking for is now archived differently, which has changed the Web address, leaving you with an error message on your screen. Don't give up hope! Here are some fictional examples to help you find what you are looking for.

You are trying to access an article called "Sit ups for Seniors." The Web address we provide is www.seniorshealth.com/article/workouts/situps.html, but alas, the address no longer works. Instead, try to access just the official website: www.seniorshealth.com (as you can see, it's just everything before and including the .*com*). It is then simple enough to just use the links on the website or a search box on the homepage to find the exact article "Sit ups for Seniors."

This strategy can be especially important for YouTube videos, because the Web addresses on YouTube are always changing but the video is almost always there.

Another option is to use a search engine (like Google.com) and type the entire title of the article "Sit ups for Seniors" (the quotation marks around it are essential for searching). See what pops up. You may find something even better than what we suggested.

MONEY MONEY MONEY! SERIES

This series highlights the financial issues your senior patrons experience and offers suggestions from locating government services to finding additional ways to earn money. As always, we place an emphasis on free or low-cost resources, speakers, and services. This series has an added bonus because of the availability of free guest speakers from government agencies and nonprofits. Part of their job is to reach out to their service group, and this is a wonderful forum for helping them do so. This series is a great place to highlight discounts for seniors ranging from travel to local businesses to education. Many seniors are eligible for such services based on financial need or simply the fact that they are over a certain age. Caregivers will benefit from finding out about these opportunities as well.

Partnerships

Local government and nonprofit groups are a prime choice for partnership. If a community partner or special guest speaker is not available for the program, a librarian can conduct a Web- or book-based program. Local restaurants and stores can be part of this series by highlighting their venue's special services for seniors through coupons, free food, and discounts.

Programs

The following is a list of programs that we have created in full for your use.

- Financial Assistance for Daily Life
- Living off the Grid/Eco-Living
- Foiling Fraud
- Second Careers
- Continuing Education
- Tax Workshop
- Retirement Finances and Fun
- Making Money the Easy Way
- Estate Planning
- Giving Back—Charities and Volunteering

Other Suggestions

Creating certain types of programming sometimes requires reliance on local resources.

Some of our best ideas need extra local flavor that only you can add, while other ideas are worth highlighting but don't need a full-length program. These ideas could function as simple links on your website or information displayed on kiosks. Here are our other suggestions:

- Local places of business with a senior discount (remind them that having an ID may be required and that they should be flattered if they are asked to show their ID)
  For example: IHOP has National Pancake Day on March 1
- Travel and recreation discounts for seniors: http://www.usa.gov/Topics/Seniors/Travel.shtml
- Legal aid
  The local Bar Association often offers a free advice night once a month. Many law firms have required pro bono hours, which often go to low-income or elderly clients. Contact your local legal aid office for the services they provide.
- Social Security: http://www.ssa.gov
  Article on age to file: http://fxn.ws/fE6qBH
- Debt (each state has different laws governing debt/declaring bankruptcy)

* * *

Program: Financial Assistance for Daily Life

Umbrella: Money Money Money! Series

Learning Goals:

1. How to find out if you qualify for all assistance programs relating to the following:
   Housing, heating, air conditioning, phone service, and food
2. How to save money on those same areas of need, even if you don't qualify

Potential Guests:

- A representative from the local housing authority
- A representative from a local utilities company

Setup Tips and Materials:

This program is more of a workshop than a presentation. The nice thing about this program is that seniors who may not qualify can still learn beneficial things for themselves and family members (who might qualify). It is also of note that property tax assistance is done on a state-by-state basis, so customize based on your own region. You will need the following:

1. Access to computers
2. Checklists and handouts that include additional resources

In-House Resources and Technology:

Books

The Moneyless Man: A Year of Freeconomic Living by Mark Boyle, ISBN 1851687815.
   The author lives a year for free!

Possum Living: How to Live Well Without a Job and with (Almost) No Money by Dolly Freed, ISBN 9780982053935.
   Find out what you need and what you don't as you continue to have the façade of a middle-class lifestyle.

Thriving During Challenging Times: The Energy, Food, and Financial Independence Handbook by Cam Mather, ISBN 0973323361.
   How to return to independence from those foundation living bills.

The Frugal Senior: Hundreds of Creative Ways to Stretch a Dollar! by Rich Gray, ISBN 9781884956492.
   A plethora of ways to stretch your money!

Free Money Free Stuff: The Select Guide to Public and Private Deals, Steals, and Giveaways by RD Editors, ISBN 9780762109036.

Websites

- U.S. Department of Housing and Urban Development (HUD): http://www.hud.gov
   HUD, "Information for Seniors": http://1.usa.gov/dYnKQn
   HUD offers information on home ownership, foreclosure prevention, housing counselors, subsidized housing, and emergency homeowner loan programs.
   State office locator: http://portal.hud.gov/hudportal/HUD?src=/localoffices
- Low Income Energy Assistance Program (LIHEAP): http://www.acf.hhs.gov/programs/ocs/liheap
   This organization provides bill payment assistance, energy crisis assistance, and even weatherization and energy-related home repairs.
- Caregiver.org: http://www.caregiver.org/caregiver/jsp/home.jsp
   Find resources by state to get assistance caring for a loved one or even yourself.

- Meals on Wheels: http://www.mowaa.org
- Federal Supplemental Nutrition Assistance Program (food stamps): http://www.fns.usda.gov/snap
    Eligibility tool: http://www.snap-step1.usda.gov/fns
- Lifeline across America: http://www.lifeline.gov/lifeline_Consumers.html
    Telephone assistance programs for low-income households provides help with starting and maintaining phone services.
- Transportation: see local and state agencies
    Learn how to qualify for free transportation, discounted public transit, and handicap parking certificates. (Check local transit authority or state department of motor vehicles for disabled parking permits.)
- Volunteers of America: http://www.voa.org/Get-Help/National-Network-of-Services/Senior_Services

Sample Presentation:

- Introduction: Be sure to mention that you will be talking about both low-income and even some high-income options on saving money.
- Speaker from a local or state government agency introduces their particular program.
- Librarian presents other local government agencies and nonprofits, detailing the services that are available. Be sure to touch on all the necessities of life (housing, food, heating, etc). Have a handout that includes all of these resources.
- Librarian presents money-saving tips and resources from in-house sources. Present a handout with all pertinent information, such as a book list.
- Speaker: Introduce a representative from a local utilities company with money-saving tips.

Additional Tools and Ideas:

Don't forget to include caregivers on this program. Put a custom advertising bookmark in all the caregiver books in the current collection. Even if the program is over, this bookmark should provide a noticeable link to the collected resources provided by the senior department on the Internet page for the program.

Promotion:

Local food banks and charities are also there to help out, so include them. The local senior center often provides at least one free meal daily, no matter one's income or assets.

Have all approved videos and Internet resources linked to a page called "Financial Assistance for Daily Life" on the senior department website. Be sure to include more than just Web address—link to lists like downloadable checklists and handouts.

Have in-house resources available for browsing one month before program. Contact all local government offices that are part of the presentation and be sure that your contacts provide you with copies (both paper and electronic) of any handouts.

Connectivity Goals:

Older adults can be isolated when in a financial slump, don't want to worry their kids, can be prideful after supporting themselves for decades without help, and may not know who to reach out to. Finances are a private thing, so connect seniors to community representatives and offer one-on-one attention, rather than a group question format. Also, have paper handouts available at all times on a kiosk so that seniors can access them discretely. Be sure to double up on all this same information on the senior department webpage.

* * *

Program: Living off the Grid—Eco-Living

Umbrella: Money Money Money! Series

Learning Goals:

1. Find out about basic living-off-the-grid concepts
2. Discover how to start living off the grid the ideal way (solar power, etc.)
3. Learn realistic ways you can reduce your reliance on the grid

Potential Guests:

- A live-off-the-grid guru with tips on how to save money through innovative living (perhaps even be a local architect who is LEED certified [Leadership in Energy and Environmental Design standards])
- Local organic urban farmer or representative from a CSA (community supported agriculture)
- Solar power installer

Setup Tips and Materials:

Self-reliance is a popular topic for this age group, so make sure that you have a focus on practical ways to apply some of these sometimes pricey concepts. (Although pricey options are really fun to learn about, if only as a possible glimpse of the future.)

You will need the following:

1. Access to computers
2. Checklists and handouts that include additional resources

In-House Resources and Technology:

Books

Living off the Grid by David Black, ISBN 9781602393165.
   This book contains basic information on reducing your carbon footprint.

The Moneyless Man: A Year of Freeconomic Living by Mark Boyle, ISBN 1851687815.
   The author lives a year for free!

Thriving During Challenging Times: The Energy, Food, and Financial Independence Handbook by Cam Mather, ISBN 0973323361.
   How to return to independence from those foundation living bills.

Articles

- Earth Easy, "What It's Like Living off the Grid," http://eartheasy.com/blog/2009/06/what-its-like-living-off-grid

Websites

- Living off the Grid: http://www.livingoffgrid.org/blog
- Off the Urban Grid: http://www.offtheurbangrid.com
   This website explores how to live in the city while living off the grid.
- Backyard Chickens: http://www.backyardchickens.com/
   This website explores raising your own poultry.

Videos

- *New York Times*, Living (mostly) off the grid: http://www.youtube.com/watch?v=3Q-6eDQ8c-A

Sample Presentation:

- Introduction: A presentation on how living off the grid can result in saving money; security if there is a services collapse; a trendy, cleaner way of living; i.e., environmentalism).
- Speaker (off-the-grid guru): This can even be a gardener who knows how to can food. Find someone who can help offset day-to-day living costs with his or her advice.
- Librarian gives a presentation from in-house resources on money-saving tips and suggests additional resources (provide handouts). Focus on *local* resources!
- Speaker: Local solar power installer, can provide a demonstration of solar panels.

Additional Tools and Ideas:

Be sure to time this program around Earth Day (April 22 of each year) for added enthusiasm and a built-in audience.

Your library should subscribe to *Consumer Reports* magazine. Sift through those and present information on the most eco-friendly cars, appliances, and even lightbulbs.

Promotion:

Have all approved videos and Internet resources linked to a page called "The Discounted Grid—Savings for Daily Living," or something similar, on the senior website. Be sure to include downloadable checklists, handouts, and forms.

Have in-house resources available for browsing one month before program.

This program could be in conjunction with Earth Day.

Connectivity Goals:

There may be some interest library wide for this program; just make sure your senior patrons get priority seating, employing the concept of concierge service for seniors.

* * *

Program: Foiling Fraud

Umbrella: Money Money Money! Series

Learning Goals:

1. Preventing phone fraud
2. Preventing mail fraud
3. Preventing door-to-door sales fraud
4. Preventing Internet fraud
5. How to avoid all other types of fraud (investments, affinity, etc.)
6. What to do if you think you were a victim of fraud

Potential Guests:

- Representative from a financial planning organization
- Representative from a local nonprofit or police force
- Representative from the local Better Business Bureau (BBB)

Setup Tips and Materials:

You will need the following:

1. Handouts
2. Projector: so patrons can be instructed in searching for businesses on the BBB website as well as on local business licensing sites.
3. Computer access

In-House Resources and Technology:

Books

Fleecing Grandma and Grandpa: Protecting against Scams, Cons, and Frauds, by Betty L. Alt and Sandra K. Wells, ISBN 0275981797.
   This book is useful for everyone, and there is a section just for Internet fraud prevention.

Scam-Proof Your Life: 377 Smart Ways to Protect You and Your Family from Ripoffs, Bogus Deals, and Other Consumer Headaches (AARP) by Sid Kirchheimer, IBSN 1402745052.
   This book includes tons of hints and tips!

The Truth about Avoiding Scams by Steve Weisman, ISBN 0132333856.
   This book is about affinity scams, where someone trusted (like a church group member) can take advantage.

Stopping Identity Theft: 10 Easy Steps to Security by Scott Mitic, ISBN 9781413309560.
   This book has an online safety focus.

Alive and Kicking: Legal Advice for Boomers by Kenney F. Hegland and Robert B. Fleming, ISBN 9781594603228.

Websites

- Save and Invest: http://www.saveandinvest.org/FraudCenter/
   This website includes free videos and info for older investors.
- USA.gov, "Consumer Protection for Seniors": http://www.usa.gov/Topics/Seniors/Consumer.shtml
   Includes information on a variety of subjects from filing a complaint on a nursing home to finding your local consumer protection office.
- AARP, "Fight Fraud": http://foundation.aarp.org/FightFraud
- National Consumers League's Fraud Center: http://www.fraud.org
   Provides numerous lists of great tips and advice sorted by types of fraud.
- Invest.gov: http://www.investor.gov
   Information on fraud avoidance, understanding fees, and research on investment products and professionals. Do a search for "fraud" on this site, there are tons of articles.

Videos

- *Helping Seniors with Finances—How to Prevent Fraud*: http://www.youtube.com/watch?v=g90JZC-uUG8
- *Protecting Older Americans from Fraud*: http://www.youtube.com/watch?v=IJTPaKli3C0
- *Richard Alderman on Identity Theft and other Scams on LIVING SMART with Patricia Gras*: http://www.youtube.com/watch?v=cRYZp_OsaPI

Sample Presentation:

- Provide an introduction to the various types of fraud.
- Librarian presents the signs of fraud.

- Speaker from the Bar Association presents on when it is appropriate to seek a lawyer.
- Librarian presents tips for preventing fraud based on in-house resources.
- Speaker from Better Business Bureau demonstrates how to use the BBB site to find out more about a business (local or national), as well as when and how to file a complaint.
- Librarian presents any additional resources and talks about handouts.

Additional Tools and Ideas:

Local and state resources are important here. Find a local nonprofit or talk to legal aid.

Often the local lawyers' Bar Association offers a free advice night or provides pro bono case work for low-income cases, like elder fraud. Most states have an office of investment securities that investigates and prosecutes fraud, frequently related to fraud against seniors.

Promotion:

Have in-house resources available for browsing one month before program. Local senior day centers and senior housing may be willing to put out fliers as well.

Have all approved videos and Internet resources linked to a page called "Foiling Fraud," or something similar, on the senior website. Be sure to include downloadable links, checklists, and handouts.

Connectivity Goals:

Help older adults get in touch with local nonprofits that can advocate for them. Make sure they know how to connect online with other consumers; they may not be aware of the huge body of reviews on companies, doctors, and nonprofits that are available online.

* * *

Program: Second Careers

Umbrella: Money Money Money! Series

Learning Goals:

1. Learn how to create an up-to-date résumé (especially digital)
2. Discover local resources for finding jobs (job service, classifieds)
3. Learn how to use technology-based networking platforms to find jobs (Monster, LinkedIn)

Potential Guests:

- A local job service office representative
- A HR or hiring officer to talk about what they look for
- Student volunteers to help with digital resume creation

Setup Tips and Materials

You will need the following:

1. Projector to show demonstrations of digital resume creation and job networking site navigation
2. Sample resumes
3. Handouts of tips
4. Handouts of recommended job sites

In-House Resources and Technology:

Books

Too Young to Retire: 101 Ways to Start the Rest of Your Life by Marika Stone, ISBN 0452285577.
    A fresh look at job seeking and finding fulfillment.

Portfolio Life: The New Path to Work, Purpose, and Passion After 50 by David D. Corbett, ISBN 078798356X.
    This book takes a look at preparing for a retirement transition by shuffling job skills to allow a meaningful pursuit at working as you age.

Websites

- Senior Community Service Employment Program (SCSEP): http://www.doleta.gov/seniors
  This site helps seniors find work through paid training (in six states currently).
- LinkedIn (find old contacts and network professionally): http://www.linkedin.com
- Monster Jobs (find jobs across the country): http://www.monster.com
- Evil HR Lady (hints and tips for interviewing): http://evilhrlady.blogspot.com
- AARP, "Work Search": http://foundation.aarp.org/WorkSearch
- Experience Works (job training and employment for seniors): http://www.experienceworks.org
- *My Retirement Blog*: http://www.myretirementblog.com

Articles

- National Council on Aging, "Mature Workers": http://www.ncoa.org/enhance-economic-security/mature-workers/

Sample Presentation:

- Introduction offers a view of the job market today.
- Librarian presents on the basics of resume creation.
- Speaker from a local job service presents the services they offer.
- Librarian presents other local job sites and Internet sites.
- Speaker from a human resources department or hiring rep volunteering to discuss interview tactics for the senior citizen.
- Librarian presents any additional resources—such as upcoming classes at the library—and talks about handouts.

Additional Tools and Ideas:

Some patrons may be just seeking work for money, while others may be seeking work for human contact and enjoyment. Be sure to take that into account.

Have lots of ideas for every skill level. Some older adults may not realize that their job skills are a bonus for them in current job types. (A former engineer may not realize that she could work part-time as an online math tutor.)

Promotion:

Have in-house resources available for browsing one month before program. Local senior day centers and senior housing may be willing to put out fliers as well.

Have all approved videos and Internet resources linked to page called "Second Careers" (or some other fun name) on the senior website. Be sure to include downloadable articles and handouts.

Connectivity Goals:

Teens and college students are also creating their first digital resumes and networking. This could be a combined multigenerational learning experience.

* * *

*Program: **Continuing Education***

Umbrella: Money Money Money! Series

Learning Goals:

1. Understand credit vs. noncredit learning
2. Learn the application process
3. Discover types and ways to finance
4. Find out other noncredit ways to continue education

Potential Guests:

- Representative from the local community college
- Adults who are continuing or pursuing their education later in life
- Someone representing the Elderhostel program

Setup Tips and Materials:

In advance, procure handouts from local colleges and education centers. Although library-made handouts with links and so forth are great, it's nice to have something professional and tangible to look at, and the colleges will be glad to provide them.

Don't forget other types of education centers like craft houses, senior centers, and even public recreation centers.

You will need the following:

1. Handouts from local colleges and education programs
2. Lists of Web links and scholarships
3. Sample college application and financial aid forms

In-House Resources and Technology:

Books

501 Ways for Adult Students to Pay for College: Going Back to School without Going Broke by Gen Tanabe and Kelly Tanabe, ISBN 9781932662337.
The Busy Adult's Guide to Making College Happen!: The Step-by-Step Guide to Finding the Time, Money, and Motivation to Complete Your College Degree by Geoffrey Schmidt, ISBN 0979869900.
Online Education for Dummies by Kevin Johnson and Susan Manning, ISBN 0470536209.

Websites

- FinAid: http://www.finaid.org
    Provides a detailed how-to with lots of explanations. Not senior specific.
- Fastweb: http://www.fastweb.com
    Fastweb is a scholarship database.
- FAFSA: http://www.fafsa.ed.gov/#
    Provides financial aid for education from the government.

Articles

- *U.S. News*, "Forget Tuition: How Retirees Can Attend College for Free": http://bit.ly/hXvLup
- *USA Today*, "Retired? Head Back to School with College Discounts": http://usat.ly/aAlcqQ

Sample Presentation:

- Introduction (educational goals): Talk about for-credit or noncredit courses and the differences in cost and ultimate result—either a degree credit or leisure learning only.
- Librarian presents information on online programs and scholarships in general, including tuition waivers, course auditing, education tax credits, noninheritable loans, Silver Scholars programs at many universities. Be sure to mention the "Senior Scholarships Program" created as part of the Edward M. Kennedy Serve America Act.
- Speaker from the local college presents the services they offer.
- Librarian presents other local educational resources (like continuing education courses offered as noncredit/entertainment by local university).
- Speaker, an older adult who has gone back and taken college classes, talks about his or her experience.
- Librarian presents any additional resources and talks about handouts.

Additional Tools and Ideas:

So many fun classes are available in many communities. Find out all the classes in your area (like at pottery shops), keep an ongoing list, and note if they offer senior discounts. For colleges and universities, find a contact whom all your senior patrons can call or email, and have his or her information readily available. Many universities have programs sponsored by the Osher Lifelong Learning Institutes, which make excellent courses available to older adults at a very low cost.

If you have senior speaker who relates his or her going back to college experience, ask if you can film the speech; it would be a great addition to the webpage for this program on the senior department website.

Promotion:

Have in-house resources available for browsing one month before program.

Have all approved Internet resources linked to a page called "Education Continued" (or some other fun name) on the senior website. Be sure to include downloadable examples and handouts.

Connectivity Goals:

If you find a great deal for a class or a great scholarship program, let your local senior centers know. That way, their patrons as well as yours can meet and participate in shared interests. Maybe you could keep in touch with attendance on popular classes and help senior patrons make new friends!

* * *

Program: Tax Workshop

Umbrella: Money Money Money! Series

Learning Goals:

1. Pretax prep: What records to save, what to toss
2. How to do taxes yourself; is it worth it?
3. Where to go for tax assistance, and discounts for seniors
4. Fun and easy tax tips and write-offs

Potential Guests:

- Speaker from a tax preparation facility
- Speaker from the local IRS office

Setup Tips and Materials

You will need the following:

1. Handouts of resources and tips
2. Example tax form filled out for a basic Social Security income tax bracket
3. A sample handout of a filled-out state tax form (assuming social security as income source)

In-House Resources and Technology:

Books

J. K. Lasser's 1001 Deductions and Tax Breaks 2011: Your Complete Guide to Everything Deductible by Barbara Weltman, IBSN 0470597240.
Taxes Made Simple: Income Taxes Explained in 100 Pages or Less, by Mike Piper, ISBN 0981454216.
Confessions of a Tax Collector: One Man's Tour of Duty Inside the IRS (P.S.) by Richard Yancey, ISBN 0060555610.
What Your CPA Isn't Telling You: Life-Changing Tax Strategies, by Mark J. Kohler, ISBN 1599184168.

Websites

- IRS, "Publications for Older Americans" and the Tax Counseling for the Elderly (TCE) Program: http://www.irs.gov/individuals/retirees/topic/index.html
  For more information on TCE call 800-829-1040.
- AARP, "AARP Foundation Tax-Aide": http://www.aarp.org/money/taxes/aarp_taxaide
  To locate the nearest AARP Tax-Aide site call 888-227-7669.
- USA.gov, "Money and Taxes for Seniors" (government hints and tips): http://www.usa.gov/Topics/Seniors/Taxes.shtml

Videos

Videos must be current to the year of the program, so here are some search tips:

- *Seniors* and *taxes* and [*year*]
- *Elderly* and *taxes* and [*year*]
- *"Tax changes"* and *seniors* and [*year*]

Sample Presentation:

- Introduction: How to get organized year-round for necessary tax information. Show sample file boxes and tips (i.e., if you donate to charity, to always get a receipt).
- Librarian discusses the pros and cons of hiring a certified public accountant (CPA) or do-it-yourself tax preparation.
- Speaker: Local CPA chimes in and gives hints and tips.
- Librarian talks about options for older adults in the community: discounts, government assistance, workshops. Also talk about hints for doing taxes yourself.
- Speaker: IRS worker offers hints and tips.
- Librarian presents any additional resources and talks about handouts.

Additional Tools and Ideas:

Taxes can make for a stressful event. Schedule this program on the same day as a fun event, like an art exhibit opening or a free concert, so patrons can unwind afterward with little effort.

Promotion:

Have in-house resources available for browsing one month before program.

Have all approved Internet resources linked to a page called "Tax Workshop" on the senior website. Be sure to include downloadable examples and handouts.

Connectivity Goals:

Have senior patrons email or write in with feedback of their tax experience and create a list of tips and reviews of CPAs to send to everyone on the email list.

* * *

Program: Retirement Finances and Fun

Umbrella: Money Money Money! Series

Learning Goals:

1. Learn about postretirement finances
2. How to make the most of your free time

Potential Guests:

- Financial planner
- An active and involved senior
- Activities planner from a local senior center
- A volunteer coordinator from a local nonprofit (or Friends of the Library)

Setup Tips and Materials:

We are going to assume that if a patron is attending a senior program that it's a bit too late for many preretirement finance planning guides, so keep the focus on postretirement finances. This is a great place to plug future programs like continuing education, hobbies that pay, and job seeking.

You will need the following:

1. Financial tips handouts
2. Books on a variety of hobbies
3. Handout with links to local classes and activities, especially those that offer a senior discount

In-House Resources and Technology:

Books

After 50 It's up to Us: Developing the Skills and Agility We'll Need by George Schofield, ISBN 9780979038242.
  Tips on how to enjoy life after 50.

Too Young to Retire: 101 Ways to Start the Rest of Your Life by Marika Stone and Howard Stone, ISBN 0452285577.
  How to turn the second half of your life into the reward it should be.

Supercharged Retirement: Ditch the Rocking Chair, Trash the Remote, and Do What You Love by Mary Lloyd, ISBN 0979831938.

The AARP Retirement Survival Guide: How to Make Smart Financial Decisions in Good Times and Bad by Julie Jason, ISBN 9781402743412.

The Joy of Not Working: A Book for the Retired, Unemployed, and Overworked—21st Century Edition by Ernie J. Zelinski, ISBN 1580085520.

How to Love Your Retirement: The Guide to the Best of Your Life by Barbara Waxman, ISBN 193351289X.

Websites

- Social Security, "How Should I Prepare for Retirement?": http://www.ssa.gov/retirement
- USA.gov, "Retirement": http://www.usa.gov/Topics/Seniors/Retirement.shtml

Articles

- *Wall Street Journal*, "Retirement 101: How to Figure Out What You'll Need": http://on.wsj.com/gaHVCc
- *AARP The Magazine*, "Retired and Loving It!": http://aarp.us/haoEPj

Sample Presentation:

- Librarian gives introduction.
- Speaker: Financial advisor speaks on postretirement financial tips.
- Librarian introduces some ideas for activities via the library resources—hobbies by book (several examples), upcoming events, ways to get involved, and volunteer opportunities.
- Speaker: Volunteer coordinator from local nonprofit or an active senior should talk about the meaning that keeping busy, engaged, and active can bring.
- Group brainstorm on local activities (have a list with resources prepared just in case).
  Examples: Be a local tourist, be a student, go to the national parks in your area, find old friends on Facebook, or become a connoisseur of something—coffee/wine/tea/fancy food/diners/sushi, etc.

Additional Tools and Ideas:

This program could be a kick-off program for your entire year's worth of programming since it is a great plug for keeping active and involved. You can also promote library-wide programming as well.

Don't forget to mention ways older adults can connect to their hobbies via the Internet through blogs, online groups, etc.

Promotion:

Have in-house resources available for browsing one month before program.

Have all approved Internet resources linked to a page called "Retirement Finances and Fun" or some other great name on the senior website. Be sure to link to upcoming programs and program websites. Senior centers would make a perfect team for this program as they can provide ready-made activities for retired seniors.

Connectivity Goals:

By connecting older patrons with an active, engaged lifestyle, you are connecting them to the community. They can build friendships, develop mentorships, and change their lives.

* * *

Program: Making Money the Easy Way

Umbrella: Money Money Money! Series

Learning Goals:

1. Learn about potential money just sitting around waiting for you
2. Discover discounts and ways to save—locally, too!
3. Find out easy, fun, and safe ways to earn money using the Internet

Potential Guests:

- Speaker who is familiar with online selling platforms such as eBay/Etsy, etc.
- Speaker who is a bargain shopper
- Speaker who is a local antiques/collectibles dealer

Setup Tips and Materials

You will need the following:

1. A projector when talking about online selling/purchasing
2. Handouts with various tips on discounts both nationally and locally
3. Handouts on eBay or Craigslist basics

In-House Resources and Technology:

Books

eBay for Seniors; Seniors for Dummies by Marsha Collier, ISBN 9780470527597.
The Complete Idiot's Guide to Making Money with Craigslist by Skip Press, ISBN 9781592579495.
eBay Photos That Sell: Taking Great Product Shots for eBay and Beyond by Dan Gookin and Robert Birnbach, ISBN 0782143814.
The Handmade Marketplace: How to Sell Your Crafts Locally, Globally, and On-Line by Kari Chapin, ISBN 9781603424776.
How to Make Money Using Etsy: A Guide to the Online Marketplace for Crafts and Handmade Products by Timothy Adam, ISBN 0470944560.
Free Stuff and Bargains for Seniors: How to Save on Groceries, Utilities, Prescriptions, Taxes, Hobbies, and More by the Editors of FC&A Publishing, ISBN 0901552569.
Amazing Insider Secrets: 1703 Money Saving Tips by Jeff Bredenberg, ISBN 9780762109838.
Frugillionaire: 500 Fabulous Ways to Live Richly and Save a Fortune by Francine Jay, ISBN 0984087303.
10,001 Ways to Live Large on a Small Budget by the Writers of Wise Bread, ISBN 160239704X.
Cheaper: Insiders' Tips for Saving on Everything by Rick Doble and Tom Philbin, ISBN 9780345512086.

Websites

- National Association of Unclaimed Property Administrators (unclaimed property website): http://www.unclaimed.org
- U.S. Department of Energy, "Program Guidance" (household rebates and government money—how to cash in): http://www1.eere.energy.gov/wip/guidance.html
- Senior Discounts (looks like a spam site, but don't be scared off): http://www.seniordiscounts.com
- AARP: http://www.aarp.org
    For $16/year, members can access an extensive list of discounts.
- Groupon: http://www.groupon.com
    Groupon is an online opportunity to obtain discounts from local businesses based on the number of people that sign up for a particular discount.
- Craigslist: http://www.craigslist.org
- Freecycle: www.freecycle.org
- eBay: www.ebay.com
- Etsy: www.etsy.com

Sample Presentation:

- Librarian provides an introduction to additional income sources.
- Librarian talks about outright free money, unclaimed money, and scholarships.

- Librarian talks about discounts.
    Main points: Always ask. Always have ID.
    Present a local and national list.
- Speaker: Local antiques dealer talks about what should be sold, what should be kept, how to tell if items from local thrift stores/garage sales are worth reselling.
- Speaker: A seller on eBay/Craigslist/Local Classifieds/Etsy talks about his or her online business and provides tips and hints.
- Librarian talks about online safety for buying and selling.

Additional Tools and Ideas:

This program is a great jumping-off point for predicting interest in future programming such as an antiques hunting or an eBay workshop. It might be fun to have a mini *Antiques Roadshow* day as a library-wide program where local antiques dealers can provide appraisals for collectibles for library patrons.

Promotion:

Have in-house resources available for browsing one month before program.

Have all approved Internet resources linked to a page called "Discounts, Bargains, and Making Extra Dough," or something similar, on the senior website. Be sure it links to upcoming program webpages on the senior department website.

Connectivity Goals:

Getting these patrons interested in bargain hunting, such as reselling items from thrift stores and garage sales, is a great way to connect them to a new hobby and to others who share their interest.

* * *

Program: Estate Planning

Umbrella: Money Money Money! Series

Learning Goals:

1. Learn about the components of an estate plan: living wills (medical directives), regular wills, trusts, and powers of attorney, etc.
2. Discover routes to creating your own estate documents.
3. Learn how to find services to assist with estate planning.

Potential Guests:

- Local attorney or lawyer
- Representative from local division of aging and adult services
- Representative from the state Bar Association's young lawyers division (many provide pro bono work for low-income patrons)

Setup Tips and Materials:

This program has a huge local component, from local free services to paid attorney services. If there is a high level of interest, it might be worth calling all the local attorneys and asking how much they charge for estate planning packages. Then confirm them on the Bar Association website, the Better Business Bureau, and online reviews. Create a final list to hand out—with a disclaimer, of course. Have a copy of your state's local health directive. Give each patron two copies: a copy for note taking and one to share with a friend or family member.

In-House Resources and Technology:

Books

Plan Your Estate by Denis Clifford, IBSN 9781413312010.
Estate Planning Smarts: A Practical, User-Friendly, Action-Oriented Guide by Deborah L. Jacobs, ISBN 9780615297545.
The 101 Biggest Estate Planning Mistakes by Herbert E. Nass, ISBN 9780470375037.
The Living Trust Advisor: Everything You Need to Know about Your Living Trust by Jeffrey L. Condon, ISBN 0470261188.
The Wall Street Journal Complete Estate-Planning Guidebook by Rachel Emma Silverman, ISBN 0307461270.

Websites

- AARP, "Estate Planning": http://www.aarp.org/money/estate-planning
- Caring Connections: http://www.caringinfo.org
     Caring Connections provides a direct link to download state-specific directives: http://www.caringinfo.org/i4a/pages/index.cfm?pageid=3289
- American Bar Association, "Estate Planning FAQs": http://bit.ly/gEB9eg
- Elder Law Answers, "Estate Planning": http://www.elderlawanswers.com/Elder_Info/Elder_Article.asp?id=703

Articles

- *CNN Money*, "Money 101 Lesson 21: Estate Planning": http://money.cnn.com/magazines/moneymag/money101/lesson21/
- *New York Times*, Your Money Guides, "Estate Planning": http://topics.nytimes.com/your-money/planning/estate-planning/index.html

Videos

- A huge series of estate planning videos are offered on YouTube by eHow: Go to www.youtube.com and search for: *ehow and "estate planning"*

Sample Presentation:

- Librarian presents an introduction defining estate planning, including all documents it entails. Show a short video.
- Speaker from the local division of aging services describes their services.
- Librarian presents which personal documents are necessary to create your estate planning package and some tips (from collection books) on how to do this process yourself.
- Speaker: Local attorney or lawyer talks about the process if patrons choose to use an attorney to create their estate planning package.
- Librarian conducts a workshop on medical directives, what each question means, and how to complete the document legally. Pass out pens and handouts for note taking.

Additional Tools and Ideas:

We have not reviewed any of the software available for creating your own estate documents. With proper review, purchasing such software might be an option for the senior department, or to forward for informational purposes to interested patrons.

Promotion:

Have in-house resources available for browsing one month before program.

Have all approved Internet resources linked to a page called "Estate Planning Workshop" (or some other great name) on the senior website.

Connectivity Goals:

Connecting patrons to the library's resources on estate planning is a great way for them to find out just how useful the library can be in their life. Any upcoming free events hosted by the local center for aging or your state's Bar Association should be listed on the website.

* * *

Program: Giving Back—Charities and Volunteering

Umbrella: Money Money Money! Series

Learning Goals:

1. Find out if volunteering is a good fit?
2. Learn about local volunteer opportunities
3. Learn how and when to give to charities
4. Learn about local charities
5. Learn how to tell if a charity is legitimate

Potential Guests:

- Friends of the Library volunteer coordinator
- Local Volunteers of America coordinator
- A guest who has done volunteer work
- A local nonprofit that accepts donations

Setup Tips and Materials:

You will need the following:

1. Projector to show computer screen
2. Handout list of *local* charities and *local* volunteer opportunities (our local department of senior services has a volunteer program, so yours might, too!)—when listing local charities, be sure to include a broad spectrum from environmental, social, and animal rescue agencies

In-House Resources and Technology:

Books

Chicken Soup for the Volunteer's Soul: Stories to Celebrate the Spirit of Courage, Caring, and Community by Jack Canfield et al., ISBN 0757300146.

Make a Difference: Your Guide to Volunteering and Community Service by Arthur I. Blaustein, ISBN 0787967890.

Wildlife and Conservation Volunteering: The Complete Guide by Peter Lynch, ISBN 1841622753.

Volunteer Vacations: Short-Term Adventures That Will Benefit You and Others by Bill McMillon et al., ISBN 9781556527845.

700 Places to Volunteer Before You Die: A Traveler's Guide by Nola Lee Kelsey, ISBN 0982549482.

Websites

- Volunteers of America: http://www.voa.org/Get-Involved/Volunteer/Get-Involved
- Senior Corps: http://www.seniorcorps.gov

- Volunteer Abroad: http://www.volunteerabroad.com/search/seniors/volunteer-abroad-1
- Peace Corps: http://multimedia.peacecorps.gov/multimedia/50plus/index.html
- HelpGuide, "Volunteering and Its Surprising Benefits": http://www.helpguide.org/life/volunteer_opportunities_benefits_volunteering.htm

Videos

- *Volunteering Keeping Seniors Healthier, Happier*: http://www.youtube.com/watch?v=Ciw2mq14DZo
- *Why Do They Do It?*—A REAL Volunteer Story: http://www.youtube.com/watch?v=Swue5ZwWpIg
- *Get Involved: Our Volunteer Stories*: http://www.youtube.com/watch?v=JD6Ne5FgeI8

Sample Presentation:

- Introduction: Should I volunteer? How to monitor volunteer time with free time; how to handle pressure you may receive to give more time than you anticipated. Patrons should always receive training from the organization for which they plan to volunteer in order to understand all the ground rules.
- Speaker from Friends of the Library regarding library volunteer opportunities. This should be a very short speech!
- Speaker from Volunteers of America presents highlights of volunteer opportunities available and how the organization can accommodate seniors' needs.
- Make time for a Q&A session with an experienced volunteer.
- Librarian presents information on charitable donations, tax info, etc.
- Librarian presents a survey of local charities and why it is so important to give to legitimate charities. Include information such as: legitimate organizations will have a tax ID number to qualify as a nonprofit, as opposed to fraudulent organizations, which will not. Be sure to stress the importance of giving locally. This is a great way to build community connections.
- Speaker from a local nonprofit speaks on the use of donated funds.
- Workshop: How to research charities; both how to find one you connect with on a personal level and how to make sure it's legitimate via the Internet.

Additional Tools and Ideas:

Try to offer snacks at this program since patrons can spend time networking with the speakers and the food can keep people lingering and visiting. Offering snacks at all senior programs is actually a good idea.

Have the teen department enlist students to make a short video, *A Day in the Life of a Senior Volunteer*, and post to the senior department website.

Intergenerational service projects, such as urban garden projects, are a great idea as well.

Promotion:

Have in-house resources available for browsing one month before program.

Have all approved Internet resources linked to a page called "Giving Back—Charities and Volunteering" or some other great identifying title on the senior department website.

Connectivity Goals:

Volunteering offers no better way for older patrons to connect to the community and each other. They connect with each other to pursue work in shared interests. They can connect to the library and other local charities. Best of all, as they volunteer they can connect with people in their community, building new friendships.

TECH BYTES TECHNOLOGY SERIES

As we learned in chapter 1, older adults are a fast-growing demographic in technology usage, particularly in the area of social networking. Technology can and should be both a useful and fun part of a senior's life. The rate of change and cost of new technology can be daunting for even a tech-savvy person. Librarians are doing their best to keep up and make technology accessible and understandable to all patrons. Library-wide programming and workshops about technology are often focused on absorbing a large amount of knowledge in a short time period. This is often because there is a need to build technology knowledge for job skills and job seeking. If there is a relevant class offered, such as Internet searching, it may move at a pace that is conducive to maximizing learning for some savvy senior patrons, but it may be daunting to others.

While it is a generalization that most seniors are new at computers, it is a safe assumption that many will want to learn at a slower pace and will have different needs and interests from persons looking for information for their junior research paper. Seniors are a dynamic, intelligent, and inquisitive age group who are ready to get into a new technology, and while they may want to skip right to the important and interesting parts, they need the background so they can repeat their efforts when they leave the library. Learning about a new technology and having a hands-on experience with it, even if they don't use the skill at home, can provide older adults with a better understanding about the world around them.

From learning how to access news events to finding the skills to keep up with their grandchild's interest in technology and discovering ways to connect with long-lost friends, technology can provide tremendous benefits to older adults. Even conversation and reading comprehension can be improved from learning the latest tech lingo as speech is growing increasingly rich with these new terms. If programming space isn't available for tech classes specific for senior patrons and you can't add any programming, then a webpage filled with links and videos that can function as tutorials should be provided on the senior department website. Additionally, a free program like Generations Online could be provided as a tutorial option (http://www.generationsonline.com). Another idea for a Tech Bytes series is to create a blog on new technology, which could be incorporated into the senior website. It could include new technology news with a spin in terms of how it could be useful specifically to these patrons.

A Word on Tech Lingo

Tech lingo examples include Wi-Fi, smartphone, iPad, tweet, blogging, de-friend, etc. Keep tech lingo to a well-explained minimum. Senior patrons will be confused if you or those training try to show off tech lingo in passing speech. When you are about to use tech lingo, try to pause and think about replacing it with a generic term or follow it up with a concise reminder/explanation. Keep any mini-lectures short and sweet, as this will help prevent the feeling that you are speaking over the patrons' heads. Providing a handout reference for these terms would be beneficial, as well.

Partnerships

Although most programs could be conducted in the computer area and, hopefully, on a projection screen in a quiet area, partnerships for increased learning can be a great asset. Arrange for mini-lessons from employees of local camera shops or local computer repair shops, computer science students from the local community college, and technology enthusiasts. This is a great place to introduce intergenerational programming. For example, teens could teach seniors for community service or even educational credits.

Programs

The following is a list of programs we have created in full for your use.

- Dealing with Digital Cameras and Photos
- Everything about Email

- Facebook: Friend or Foe
- Blogging Basics
- Genealogy, It's in the Genes
- Online Shopping Know-How
- Trip Planning Online
- Surfing for Seniors—Internet Basics Workshop
- Online Entertainment
- Digital Books and E-Readers

Other Suggestions

Creating programming sometimes requires reliance on local resources. Some of our great ideas need extra local flavor that only you can add, while other ideas are worth highlighting but don't need a full-length program. These ideas could function as simple links on your website or information displayed on kiosks.

- E-cards
- Digital video camera workshop
- Creating YouTube videos
    Peter Oakley is an example of a senior who became famous for his videos. His YouTube channel is called *The Internet Grandad*. You can also find him by his username: *geriatric* 1927.
    Here is a list of his YouTube videos: http://www.youtube.com/user/geriatric1927#p/u
    Here is an article about him from the *UK Telegraph* titled "83-year-old YouTube star leads way online": http://bit.ly/ivruCh
- Scanning workshop
- How to rev up your hobby with the Internet (forums, local links)
- How to create a free website (if there is interest in taking technology this far): Recommend: http://www.webs.com

* * *

Program: Dealing with Digital Cameras and Photos

Umbrella: Tech Bytes

Learning Goals:

1. Find out what digital cameras can do and how they work
2. Discover how to choose a digital camera
3. Learn how a digital camera and computer work together
4. Find out how to store, save, send, and get photos ready for printing
5. Try out editing photos for fun

Potential Guests:

- Photo shop owner
- Photography buff
- Photography class students from local high school or university
- Graphic artist

Setup Tips and Materials:

You will need the following:

1. A projector so that patrons can see an example computer screen and photo editing before they try it out at the computer stations or in the computer lab

2. Computer station
3. A selection of digital cameras
4. A CD containing photos as an example
5. A projection screen
6. Instructional handouts
7. A handout listing local photo classes and photo clubs for older patrons

In-House Resources and Technology:

Books

Really, Really, Really Easy Step-by-Step Digital Photography: For Absolute Beginners of All Ages by Gavin Hoole
and Cheryl Smith, ISBN 9781845372453.
David Pogue's Digital Photography: The Missing Manual by David Pogue, ISBN 0596154038.
How to Do Everything Digital Photography by Jason R. Rich, ISBN 0071754717.
Picasa for Seniors: Get Acquainted with Picasa: Free, Easy-to-Use Photo Editing Software (Computer Books for
Seniors series) by Studio Visual Steps, ISBN 9789059052468.

Websites (Informational)

- How Stuff Works, "Digital Cameras": http://bit.ly/boZeZl
- Digital Photography Tips: http://www.digital-photography-tips.net/digital-photography-tutor.html#tutorials
- Beginner Photography Guide: http://www.beginner-photography-guide.com
- Digital Photography School, "11 Tips for Beginner Photographers": http://www.digital-photography-school.com/11-tips-for-beginner-photographers

National Photo Printing/Sharing Websites

- Kodak Gallery: http://www.kodakgallery.com/gallery/welcome.jsp
- Snapfish: http://www.snapfish.com/snapfish/welcome
- Shutterfly: http://www.shutterfly.com

Photo Editing Websites

Free

- SumoPaint (our favorite!): http://www.sumopaint.com/home
- Picasa (also provides photo sharing): http://picasa.google.com
- Splashup: http://www.splashup.com
- Dr. Pic: http://www.drpic.com
- FotoFlexer: http://fotoflexer.com
- LunaPic (includes a fun animation creator): http://www.lunapic.com/editor
- Pixenate: http://pixenate.com
- Gimp (more complex but a good resource for an experienced digital editor): http://www.gimp.org

Costs but Worth It

- Adobe Photoshop Elements
  This program is basic, fun, and easy to use. Can be used for more than photo editing—including creating fliers and posters in a pinch, such as a poster for a lost pet or a garage sale flyer.

Videos

- *Henry's Cameras—How to Choose a Digital Camera*: http://www.youtube.com/watch?v=1Jg2XG5lxlw
- *PC World: How to Buy a Digital Camera*: http://www.youtube.com/watch?v=DRjb3Ju7Wu4
- *VideoJug: How to Choose a Digital Camera*: http://www.youtube.com/watch?v=6xad3uvFYqQ
- Littlegemsphoto. How to upload pictures to your computer from your camera: http://www.youtube.com/watch?v=XbWAGULSonM

Sample Presentation:

- Librarian introduces digital cameras. Addresses questions such as the following:
  Are they necessary? (No, regular camera film can be easily processed into digital photos at a photo shop.) Do you need a computer to have a digital camera? (No, they can be printed right off the camera at a photo shop and saved on a CD for later reprints.)
- Speaker: A camera shop owner describes how to choose a camera that is right for you.
  Factors to consider: complexity, size, button size, and memory.
- Librarian presents how to use your digital camera in conjunction with a computer.
  Topics include where to save file, how to download, how to delete photos off the camera, and archive methods.
- Speaker: A graphic artist explains how to use free online programs to do basic photo edits and how to finalize preparing them for printing (most digital photos must be resized to print correctly).
- Librarian speaks on local photos shops and the discounts they offer.
- Workshop: Digital photos from start to finish! Each senior goes through the entire digital process: turn on camera, choose settings, take a photo, download to computer, erase off camera, basic photo edits, and how to send to a printer or burn to a disc to take to printer.

Additional Tools and Ideas:

It is essential that the library have a set of 5–10 digital cameras available for in-library use by all for demonstrations and projects. Others should be available just for librarians and staff so they can record events and programs for print or by posting them on the website. If cameras are available for in-library use or checkout, a senior photo essay project would be an amazing display for the senior area or library gallery. It could include photos of day-to-day life or simply show images that caught patrons' eyes in and around the library. Printing donations could be solicited from a local printing store, perhaps framing from a frame shop. Voilà, a new hobby is born!

Promotion:

Have in-house resources available for browsing one month before program.

Have all approved Internet resources linked to a page called "Dealing with Digital Cameras and Photos" on the senior department website. Include samples of edited photos taken in house, with permission.

Connectivity Goals:

Photography has become much easier, but digital cameras can be daunting. By educating older patrons to this new technology, interest in photography can be reawakened or simply introduced. Connecting these patrons to a meaningful hobby will allow them to make friends and interact with the community.

This program is perfect for intergenerational programming for teens and seniors. They can learn together, or the teens could teach the seniors. They could combine efforts and create an art show together. "Teen Daily Life" juxtaposed with "Senior Daily Life" would be interesting to show the challenging side of being a teen and the fun side of being a senior, such as images of teens in a classroom while the lucky seniors play golf.

* * *

Program: Everything about Email

Umbrella: Tech Bytes

Learning Goals:

1. Discover what email is
2. Learn how to choose and set up a free email account (or two)
3. Discover how to use email
4. Learn about email etiquette
5. Learn about email safety and spam

Potential Guests:

The librarian can run this whole workshop like a pro!

Setup Tips and Materials:

You will need the following:

1. A projector so that patrons can see examples on a computer screen
2. Have patrons who sign up in advance bring with them the email addresses of their close friends and family
3. Access to computers
4. Handouts with instructions

In-House Resources and Technology:

Books

Send: Why People Email So Badly and How to Do It Better by David Shipley and Will Schwalbe, ISBN 0307270602.
E-Mail for Dummies by John R. Levine et al., ISBN 0764501313.

Websites

- Gmail (a free online email and much more): http://www.gmail.com
- Hotmail (a free online email): http://www.hotmail.com
- *Wikipedia*, "Comparison of Webmail Providers": http://en.wikipedia.org/wiki/Comparison_of_webmail_providers
- Yahoo Directory: Free Email. A list of free Web email providers: http://bit.ly/i8AZnP

Articles

- eHow, "How to Use Email": http://www.ehow.com/how_4477916_use-email.html
- A Beginner's Guide to Effective Email: http://webfoot.com/advice/email.top.php
- Sticksite: Email Help: A list of email tips: http://www.sticksite.com/email.html

Videos

- *Yahoo Email Raw Basics, for Beginners*: http://www.youtube.com/watch?v=4_aq8ZnuijI
- *Google Email Raw Basics, for Beginners*: http://www.youtube.com/watch?v=eGH0ZaBxmwI

Sample Presentation:

As this is a workshop, this presentation can be done in a lecture format or step by step at individual computers.

- Introduction: Describe what email is and its benefits.
- Present the options for setting up a free email account. Have patrons create two emails accounts: one for friends and family, which can have part or all of their real name in it. They should never sign up for a shopping or email list with this account. Having your real name on an account increases the chances for spam. The other account is the one to use for shopping and other online activities, and should be fancifully named. Give examples of when to use one or the other.
- Present how to use email, step by step: how to remember login passwords; how to create, send, forward, and reply; how to attach documents and photos; and how to archive and retrieve old emails. A priority is to talk about how to log out, especially on public computers.
- Provide a brief chat about email etiquette. Emphasize that it is a problem when people are too abrupt and that the written word can be taken the wrong way. Include these topics: As with any written communication, it is important to address all questions asked. Don't forward junk mail, joke mail, or spam. Never give out someone's email address without asking them first. When forwarding an item, clear out prior senders' information.
- Discuss email safety and spam issues, such as: Never download documents from unknown sources. Never ever reply to spam emails. If you don't recognize an email, look at its properties, and if it still looks unfamiliar, delete it unopened.

Additional Tools and Ideas:

If the group is moving along fast enough, e-card creation and sending can be introduced. Many free email programs, like Gmail, offer other interesting features worth exploring. Make sure to sign seniors up for the senior department's email list for updates and special opportunities from the library.

Promotion:

Marketing for this program is essential since it can be hard to imagine how beneficial email can be if a person doesn't understand email and its uses. Be sure to catch their attention with a list of benefits on the website and fliers.

Stay connected with your grandchildren!
Stay connected to your business associates!
Stay connected to your favorite products!
Send and receive computer documents and photos with ease!

Have in-house resources available for browsing one month before program.
Have all approved Internet resources linked to a page called "All about Email" on the senior department website. Include links to signing up for email updates from a variety of library departments.

Connectivity Goals:

As a connective tool used properly, email can be a great way for seniors to connect with their friends, family, and the community.

This program is perfect for intergenerational programming for teens and seniors. They can learn together, or the teens could teach the older adults.

* * *

Program: Facebook—Friend or Foe?

Umbrella: Tech Bytes

Learning Goals:

1. Discuss whether Facebook is right for you
2. Learn how to set up a Facebook account

3. Learn how to use a Facebook account
4. Discuss safety and other concerns

Potential Guests:

- Intergenerational programming using teens from the library
- A Facebook addict

Setup Tips and Materials:

You will need the following:

1. Access to computers
2. A projector to show a computer screen
3. Handouts with instructions

In-House Resources and Technology:

Books

Facebook and Twitter for Seniors for Dummies by Marsha Collier, ISBN 0470637544.
The Facebook Guide for People over 50 by Paul McFedries, ISBN 0470875178.
Facebook for Grown-Ups by Michael Miller, ISBN 078974712X.
The Facebook Effect: The Inside Story of the Company That Is Connecting the World by David Kirkpatrick, ISBN 1439102120.

Websites

- Facebook: http://www.facebook.com
- Eons.com, a social networking site for boomers (as an alternative to Facebook): http://www.eons.com

Articles

- AllAssistedLivingHomes.com, Facebook Infographic, "Senior Citizens: The New Facebook User": http://bit.ly/baNN46
- Wikihow, "How to Teach Facebook to Seniors": http://www.wikihow.com/Teach-Facebook-to-Seniors
- Facebook for Beginners: http://hubpages.com/hub/facebookforbeginners
- Atlantic.com, "Facebook for Centenarians: Senior Citizens Learn Social Media" by Aylin Zafar: http://bit.ly/qOtHpw

Movies

- *The Social Network* (2011) directed by David Fincher, starring Jesse Eisenberg, Andrew Garfield, Justin Timberlake, et al. (If showing as part of the program, carefully select scenes because parts of this movie are not appropriate for public display.)

Videos

- *Grandma on Facebook*: http://www.youtube.com/watch?v=XRIfTaBbkvY
- *Facebook and Social Media for Senior Citizens*: http://www.youtube.com/watch?v=utnxz_L98Dg
- *How to Create a Facebook Account*: http://www.youtube.com/watch?v=vBBnZsH1rpE
- *The Graying of Social Networks*: http://www.youtube.com/watch?v=CS2_1ttOodI

- *Facebook for Beginners Revised by Mark Ellis*: http://www.youtube.com/watch?v=l6bO_hbMEBk
- *Senior Lifestyles: Savvy Seniors Using Facebook* (audio only): http://www.youtube.com/watch?v=m0f Dhier4LM
- *How to Set Up Privacy Settings*: http://www.youtube.com/watch?v=WXK7B6Aln8c

Sample Presentation:

- Librarian introduces Facebook and discusses reasons to have a Facebook page.
- Librarian shows off the library's Facebook page or his or her personal page.
- Speaker: Facebook guru or college student goes over the basics of how to set up a page, discusses what privacy/safety means on Facebook, and demonstrates how to use the account.
- Workshop: Intergenerational programming. Teens come in to coach seniors in how to set up an account, or students setting up their first account can join for a workshop.

Additional Tools and Ideas:

Allow seniors to come in anytime for assistance with Facebook, from scanning and uploading photos to de-friending advice. Gauge interest in other social networking tools like LinkedIn for future programming.

A great new option for an alternative to Facebook is called Google+: https://plus.google.com/. Here's an article with more information:

Mashable, "Google+ the Complete Guide": http://mashable.com/2011/07/16/google-plus-guide

Promotion:

Marketing for this program is essential since it can be hard to imagine how beneficial Facebook can be if a person doesn't understand its uses. Be sure to catch attention with lists of benefits on the website and fliers.

Stay connected with your grandchildren!
Stay connected to your business associates!
Stay connected to your favorite businesses and products!

Have in-house resources available for browsing one month before the program.
Have all approved Internet resources linked to a page called "Facebook: Friend or Foe" on the senior department website.

Connectivity Goals:

As a connective tool used properly, Facebook can be a great way for seniors to connect with their friends, family, and the community.

This program is perfect for intergenerational programming for teens and senior patrons. They can learn together, or the teens could teach the seniors.

* * *

Program: Blogging Basics

Umbrella: Tech Bytes

Learning Goals:

1. Understanding blogs
2. How to follow a blog
3. How to set up a free blog of your own

4. How to create blog postings
5. Learn about safety and privacy issues

Potential Guests:

- An avid blogger

Setup Tips and Materials:

You will need the following:

1. Access to computers
2. A projector to show a computer screen
3. Handouts with instructions

In-House Resources and Technology:

Books

Blogging All-in-One for Dummies by Susan Gunelius, ISBN 9780470573778.
Creative Blogging: Your First Steps to a Successful Blog by Heather Wright-Porto, ISBN 9781430234289.
No One Cares What You Had for Lunch: 100 Ideas for Your Blog by Margaret Mason, ISBN 032144972X.

Websites

- Blogger (free blog creator): http://www.blogger.com
- LiveJournal (free blog creator): www.livejournal.com
- Posterous (free blog creator): https://posterous.com
- Wordpress (free blog creator): http://wordpress.org
- TypePad (free blog creator): http://www.typepad.com
- Google Reader (blog reader): http://www.google.com/reader

Articles

- Electronic Frontier Foundation: "Legal Guide for Bloggers": http://www.eff.org/issues/bloggers/legal
    "How to Blog Safely": http://www.eff.org/wp/blog-safely
- About.com, "Top 10 Reasons to Blog": http://weblogs.about.com/od/startingablog/tp/Top-Ten-Reasons-to-Blog.htm
- *USA Today*, "Senior Citizen Bloggers Defy Stereotypes": http://www.usatoday.com/tech/news/2005-11-06-geezer-blog_x.htm

Example Blogs

- *Mature Not Senile*: http://jude8753.com
- *Style Crone*: http://stylecrone.com
- Henry Alford's Top 10 Blogs by or about Senior Citizens: http://bit.ly/k1d1cU

Videos (should be customized to the blogging host you choose to highlight)

- Atomic Learning, "Blogging Workshop" (video tutorials specifically for Blogger): http://www.atomiclearning.com/k12/blogging
- *Blogger Tutorial: How to Start Blogging with Blogger*: http://www.youtube.com/watch?v=ryb4VPSmKuo
- *How to Blog Using Wordpress*: http://www.youtube.com/watch?v=hg6XUX48Q1M

Sample Presentation:

- Librarian introduces the concept of a blog. Show example blogs such as the library senior department blog that you have recently created and are updating daily!
- Librarian shows how a blog reader (a program that collects in one easy place all the new posts of all the blogs you want to follow) works, how to search and find blogs, and how to add them to the reader.
- Guest speaker: An avid blogger shows off a blog creator of choice and explains why people blog. Emphasis is on the interaction with readers and how it has benefited them.
- Librarian presents some safety and privacy tips. For example: Bet you didn't know that photos taken with a GPS-containing phone stamp the photo with the coordinates of where you took the photo. That way everyone on the Internet can find out exactly where you live via that photo you took of your new big-screen TV.
- Workshop: How to make a blog and create posts.

Additional Tools and Ideas:

Have seniors send you links to their active blogs so they can be showcased on the library website or senior department website.

Provide links to famous blogs created by older adults.

Promotion:

Marketing for this program is essential since it can be hard to imagine how fun blogging can be if a person doesn't understand its uses. Be sure to catch attention with lists of benefits on the website and fliers.

Show off your skills and talents!
Share your interests!
Share your thoughts and knowledge!
Make money!

Have in-house resources available for browsing one month before program.

Have all approved Internet resources linked to a page called "Blogging Basics" on the senior department website.

Have any digital photo workshops conducted sometime *after* this program so you can refer interested patrons to attend.

Connectivity Goals:

Following blogs and creating one of your own are great ways for senior patrons to connect with a worldwide community that shares their interests.

* * *

Program: Genealogy, It's in the Genes

Umbrella: Tech Bytes

Learning Goals:

1. Find a good starting place for doing genealogy
2. Find free websites that aid the genealogy process
3. Find fee-based websites that aid the genealogy process
4. Discover how to network and share findings
5. Discuss the place of genetics and genetic testing in genealogy

Potential Guests:

- A genealogy guru
- Someone who has taken a genetic ancestry test

Setup Tips and Materials:

It is important to have someone who has gone through this process with examples prepared to show on a projected computer screen. For example, if they used a free family tree creator, they can show what the final product looked like.

You will need the following:

1. Access to computers
2. A projector to show a computer screen
3. Handouts with instructions

In-House Resources and Technology:

Books

The Everything Guide to Online Genealogy: Use the Web to Trace Your Roots, Share Your History, and Create a Family Tree by Kimberly Powell, ISBN 1440511683.
Collecting Dead Relatives: An Irreverent Romp through the Field of Genealogy by Laverne Galeener-Moore, ISBN 0806311819.
Genealogy Online 9/E by Elizabeth Crowe, ISBN 0071740376.
Secrets of Tracing Your Ancestors by W. Daniel Quillen, ISBN 9781593601386.
Shaking the Family Tree: Blue Bloods, Black Sheep, and Other Obsessions of an Accidental Genealogist by Buzzy Jackson, IBSN 9781439112991.
Crash Course in Genealogy by David Dowell, ISBN 9781598849394.

Magazine

- *Family Tree* magazine (also lots of content on their website): http://www.familytreemagazine.com

Websites

- Ancestory.com is fee-based, but it also offers a 14-day free trial: http://www.ancestry.com
  There is a free site by the same company that includes many free tools like charts and a free searchable Social Security death index: http://www.rootsweb.ancestry.com
- Family Search.org (free): https://www.familysearch.org/
- USGenWeb Project (free) includes a state-by-state resource guide: http://usgenweb.org
- My Heritage (free): http://www.myheritage.com
  Features a family website creator for sharing family tree, photos, and more.
- Cyndi's List (lists many links on a variety of genealogy topics): http://www.cyndislist.com
- U.S. Government National Archives: http://www.archives.gov/research/genealogy/index.html
- National Geographic Gene Testing Kit: http://bit.ly/dV1Fxa
- Genetic Testing Laboratories Gene Testing Kit: http://bit.ly/gea3Bv
- 23andme Genetic Testing (has a wonderful connectivity component—allows you, with permission, to find people to whom you are genetically related and compare traits and even health!): https://www.23andme.com

Articles

- The DNA Testing Advisor: http://www.dna-testing-adviser.com/index.html

Videos

- *Genealogy #01: Beginning Your Family Tree*: http://www.youtube.com/watch?v=Rk2RVQBLrq4
- *The Joy of Genealogy and Family History*: http://www.youtube.com/watch?v=btjPbRFaK24
- *The Generations Project* (a reality series of real people seeking their past, episodes can be accessed online for free): http://www.byutv.org/thegenerationsproject
- Yourgenome: *Over the Counter Testing*: http://www.youtube.com/watch?v=GMzTUsffU1g
- NBC TV series *Who Do You Think You Are*: http://www.nbc.com/who-do-you-think-you-are/

This fun show explores the genealogical history of celebrities.

Sample Presentation:

- Librarian introduces genealogy and how it can be interesting and fun.
  Start with what you know, organize it, and prepare to do research from there.
- Share a video clip from the NBC TV series *Who Do You Think You Are?* http://www.nbc.com/who-do-you-think-you-are/
- Librarian presents free websites with genealogy tools and tips.
- Speaker: Genealogy gurus present their preferred websites, especially their reviews of those that cost money, as well as how they have networked and shared their discoveries.
- Librarian presents other ways to network and share, perhaps a locked family blog or website. Also discusses options for genetic testing to find out ancient ancestry. If you can, find a guest speaker who has taken the test.

Additional Tools and Ideas:

It would be interesting to have a regular patron or even a librarian blog about his or her search, uploading found photos and generic information to illustrate the journey. Or a staff member could be allowed to do this with their own genealogy (on the clock during slow times), provided they are willing to share their process and some results publicly.

If senior patrons want to go the extra mile, help them out with library tools. Video or voice recordings of their memories of long-deceased relatives can be made at the library and uploaded to their website or blog.

Local historical societies and state organizations such as a state archive or state history museum frequently provide genealogy workshops as part of their mission. You might find a free presenter from one of these organizations.

Promotion:

Have in-house resources available for browsing one month before your program. It is important that patrons see how much the library can offer by way of historical and country information that will help flesh out their ancestor search.

Have all approved Internet resources linked to a page called "Genealogy, It's in the Genes" on the senior department website.

Have any digital photo workshops conducted sometime *after* this program so you can encourage interested patrons to attend.

Connectivity Goals:

An avid interest in a hobby such as tracing one's ancestry is a great way for senior patrons to connect with each other. Genealogy is a natural way for patrons to connect with their families, so it is important to provide a variety of sharing tools, like printable family tree charts. Reconnecting to the past and what you learn from it should be shared. Allow participating patrons to record oral histories by video or audio, have an exhibit of family trees or family photographs as a project, or share an exhibit with a local senior center or historical society. Check for local genealogy clubs as well. They really do exist, even in small towns or rural areas.

* * *

Program: Online Shopping Know-How

Umbrella: Tech Bytes

Learning Goals:

1. Find out if online shopping is right for you
2. Learn how to identify a reliable online shop
3. Learn how to use online shopping sites for your benefit
4. Find out how to keep your personal and credit card information safe while shopping online

Potential Guests:

• A patron or librarian with a cautionary online shopping story

Setup Tips and Materials:

You will need the following:

1. Access to computers
2. A projector to show a computer screen
3. Handouts with instructions

In-House Resources and Technology:

Books

The Secrets to Online Bargain Shopping: Money Saving Ideas and Tips for Finding Bargain Deals on the Internet by K M S Publishing.com, ISBN 1452894884.
The Internet Angel: The Best 1000 Discount Websites by Annie Challis, ISBN 057801470X.
The Complete Idiot's Guide to eBay, 2nd Edition by Lissa McGrath and Skip McGrath, ISBN 1592579698.
Using the Internet Safely for Seniors for Dummies by Nancy C. Muir and Linda Criddle, ISBN 0470457457.

Websites

• Safe Shopping (by the American Bar Association): http://www.safeshopping.org
• Better Business Bureau, "Online Shopping Tips": http://files.intra.bbb.org/OnlineShopTips/tips.asp
• Privacy Rights Clearinghouse: "Fact Sheet 23: Online Shopping Tips: E-Commerce and You": http://www.privacyrights.org/fs/fs23-shopping.htm
• Paypal keeps your personal information so you don't have to provide it to every site. Some sites require you have a Paypal account: http://www.paypal.com
• Have examples of your favorite primary purchase website—perhaps a major bookseller—and your favorite secondary purchase site (eBay). Find a site you don't trust to show as an example as well.

Videos

• *MacMost Now 10: Online Shopping Safety*: http://bit.ly/GDCvCk
• *Online Shopping: BBC Watchdog*: http://www.youtube.com/watch?v=4LSnVYUbrzI

- *Expert Tops for Online Shopping Safety and Bargain Hunting*: http://www.youtube.com/watch?v=Yvt6 Penic0g

Sample Presentation:

- Librarian introduces online shopping and talks about experiences with online purchasing and shopping. You don't need to make purchases to obtain benefits, but if you do make purchases, you need an email account and a credit/debit card.
- Librarian talks about how to easily identify legitimate shops (a national or well-known company or through word of mouth) or how to tell with some leg work, such as looking up the business license and home location. Also suggest buying from U.S. or Canadian companies for cheaper shipping and better chance of legitimacy.
- Librarian talks about how to use online shopping to your benefit: reviews on products, finding it locally, price comparison shopping, upcoming products, and preordering for a discount. You can order some items online only and have them delivered for free to a local store for pickup, such as Walmart and many photo sites.
- Librarian talks about safety: Step 1: Check credibility of an online shopping venue. Step 2: Obtain a second dedicated debit or credit card so your primary account is safe. Step 3: Check for encryption. If you don't see "https://" in the browser address window, don't enter your personal information. Step 4: Choose to create an account or to purchase without a formal account. Additionally, discuss the difference between buying from a private person (used on Amazon Marketplace, eBay, Etsy) vs. from a company. Understand consumer rights. Discuss placing phone orders vs. online ordering. Most legitimate websites have phone ordering info posted so you can just call in your order instead. This way, patrons avoid typing private information online. By providing the company with an email address, patrons can receive a receipt and tracking information via email.
- Closing remarks: If you use reviews for products online, be sure to create and post them, too!

Additional Tools and Ideas:

Librarians really shouldn't recommend specific shopping sites due to liability issues and the nonprofit status of most libraries, but if a shopping website has a service that endears itself to older people in the community, it can and should be highlighted. For example, online sites with senior discounts or even local grocery store sites that offer home delivery could be part of a presentation. Just be sure everyone knows you aren't asking or suggesting that they shop at a particular site, you are just making them aware of the site. Shopping there would be entirely up to the individual.

Promotion:

Have in-house resources available for browsing one month before program.

Have all approved Internet resources linked to a page called "Online Shopping Know-How" on the senior department website.

Connectivity Goals:

Online shopping is about more than just a purchase; it empowers buyers by connecting them to a broad range of information. In the past, buyers were at the mercy of the local supply and word of mouth. Buyers today can read worldwide reviews and make their own; they can check if a business is legitimate, price compare, and make better informed decisions.

* * *

Program: Trip Planning Online

Umbrella: Tech Bytes

Learning Goals:

1. Find out if trip planning online is right for you
2. Discover some great sites for trip planning
3. Learn how to use reviews, ratings, refunds, and discounts
4. Learn how the using the Web can be different from working with a travel agent

Potential Guests:

- A local travel agent(s)
- A patron/librarian who is willing to share his or her experiences

Setup Tips and Materials:

You will need the following:

1. Access to computers
2. A projector to show a computer screen
3. Handouts with instructions

In-House Resources and Technology:

Books

Great Age Guide to Online Travel by Sandy Berger, ISBN 0789735717.
The Traveler's Web: An Extreme Searcher Guide to Travel Resources on the Internet by Randolph Hock, ISBN 9780910965750.
The Red Hat Society Travel Guide: Hitting the Road with Confidence, Class, and Style by Thomas Nelson, ISBN 1401603645.
The Boomers' Guide to Going Abroad to Travel | Live | Give | Learn by Doris Gallan, ISBN 160910630X.
Grandma Needs a Four-Wheel Drive: Adventure Travel for Seniors by Janet Webb Farnsworth and Bernadette Heath, ISBN 1604945575.
How to Travel Practically Anywhere by Susan Stellin, ISBN 9780618607532.
Make Your Travel Dollars Worth a Fortune: The Contrarian Traveler's Guide to Getting More for Less by Tim Leffel, ISBN 9781932361391.
Lonely Planet The Travel Book by Lonely Planet, ISBN 9781741792119.
Journeys of a Lifetime: 500 of the World's Greatest Trips by National Geographic, ISBN 1426201257.

Websites

- Travel Channel: Create a great idea list for vacations, like Haunted Travels! http://www.travelchannel.com/Places_Trips
- Expedia: http://www.expedia.com
- Travelocity: http://www.travelocity.com
- Trip Advisor: http://www.tripadvisor.com
- Google Maps: Look up any business with their name or address and read reviews: http://www.google.com/maps
- Orbitz: http://www.orbitz.com
- Travel Muse: A great free travel planner/organizer—save sites, collaborate, and share: http://www.travelmuse.com

Articles

- 50 Something, "Destination Guides": http://www.50something.us/modules.php?name=Travel
  Includes a detailed travel section with reviews by people over the age of 50.
- Suite101, "Senior Travel": http://www.suite101.com/seniortravel
- AARP, "Travel": http://www.aarp.org/travel
- *Travel with Grandma: Tips for Traveling with the Frail Elderly*: http://www.travelwithgrandma.blogspot.com
- *USA Today*, "Travel Tips for the Elderly": http://traveltips.usatoday.com/travel-tips-elderly-13507.html
- More with Less Today, "Travel Discounts for Seniors": http://morewithlesstoday.com/travel-discounts-for-seniors
  Lists major travel companies that offer a senior discount.
- Home Exchange 50 Plus: http://www.homeexchange50plus.com
- Walking the World: http://www.walkingtheworld.com
- Road Scholar: All-inclusive moderately priced education travel for adults featuring project and sites around the world: http://www.roadscholar.org

Sample Presentation:

- Librarian provides introduction to three options: Trip planning via phone, using a travel agent, or using online resources and booking.
- Speaker: Travel agents discuss their current place in the industry, how can they help, how much they cost, and why they are valuable.
- Librarian presents an overview of the best/easiest to use trip-planning sites. These can include official state and country websites as well.
- Librarian presents an example vacation and demonstrates how to research the trip using reviews and ratings, ending with a list of travel businesses offering a senior discount.
- Librarian presents a quick talk about online safety. This includes a review of online credit card use and how to read fine print for refund information.
- Librarian conducts a mini-workshop where each patron researches a place he or she would like to go or an upcoming trip.

Additional Tools and Ideas:

Hobbies can be made into themed vacations. For example: if your hobby section on golf is popular, obtain some golf vacation guides or a list of sites for the website. Other ideas: great food, genealogy, wine, best beaches, religious, RV travel.

If you have an active patron body, you may want to promote the latest craze of learning/volunteer/eco-tourism. Here are some examples:

Earthwatch Institute: http://www.earthwatch.org/expedition
Choice Humanitarian: http://choicehumanitarian.org/expeditions.php
Natural Habitat Adventure: http://www.nathab.com
World Wildlife: http://www.worldwildlife.org/travel/index.html
Volunteer Guide: http://volunteerguide.org/volunteer/vacations.htm
Book: *Volunteer Vacations Across America: Immersion Travel USA* by Sheryl Kayne. ISBN 0881508640

Another idea is to do a mini-workshop on YouTube video finding: patrons could look up a place they want to travel and watch feedback or vacation videos that people have posted.

Promotion:

Have in-house resources available for browsing one month before program.

Have all approved Internet resources linked to a page called "Trip Planning Online" on the senior department website.

Connectivity Goals:

Reviewing and sharing feedback on travel experiences empowers seniors by connecting them to a broad range of information. Travelers today can read worldwide reviews and make their own reviews. They can check if a business is legitimate, price compare, and make better informed decisions.

* * *

Program: Surfing for Seniors—Internet Basics Workshop

Umbrella: Tech Bytes

Learning Goals:

1. Learn about what Web browsers are and the different options available
2. Learn what a direct IP addresses is
3. Discover search engines
4. Learn about hyperlinks and how to open new windows
5. Find out tricks, such as saving favorites and security

Potential Guests:

- Intergenerational: Local high school computer club where students teach older patrons
- Intergenerational: Children's department patrons where everyone learns together
- Tech guru

Setup Tips and Materials:

You will need the following:

1. Access to computers
2. A projector to show a computer screen
3. Handouts with instructions

In-House Resources and Technology:

Books

The Senior's Guide to Easy Computing: PC Basics, Internet, and E-Mail (Senior's Guide series) by Rebecca Sharp Colmer, ISBN 0965167208.
Is This Thing On?: A Late Bloomer's Computer Handbook by Abby Stokes, ISBN 0761146199.
Absolute Beginner's Guide to Computer Basics (5th Edition) by Michael Miller, ISBN 9780789742537.
Computing for Seniors in Easy Steps: For the Over 50s by Sue Price, ISBN 9781840782905.

Websites

- *PC World*, "Learn the Basics of Web Browser Security": http://bit.ly/hiCDYI
- Goodwill Community Foundation, LearnFree.org, "Internet Basics" (tutorials): http://www.gcflearnfree.org/internet
- Internet Basics Bee: http://www.basicsbee.com/lesson1.html
- Internet 101: http://www.internet101.org
- Basics for Beginners: http://www.basics4beginners.com

Videos

- *Internet for Seniors: A Step-by-Step Guide for the Computer Shy*
  Available on Amazon. 120 Minutes.
- *Senior Computer Lesson 1*: http://www.youtube.com/watch?v=9Z1VOEnDhhc
- *Web Search Strategies in Plain English*: http://www.youtube.com/watch?v=B8aYoVpdz8o
  This series is great; check out their other videos, too!
- *Creating Better Internet Searches*: http://www.youtube.com/watch?v=p9hwC4nvKJE
- Meganga, Free Basic Computer Training: http://www.meganga.com/category/free-lessons

Sample Presentation:

- Librarian provides introduction to how being able to effectively navigate the Internet is the key to opening up new worlds.
- Speaker: Tech guru talks about Web browsers and how to choose the best one for you.
  Workshop begins using the library's chosen Web browser. (At this point a local high school computer class of teens pair ups with seniors.)
- Students demonstrate how to use a direct IP address.
- Students demonstrate their search engine of choice.
- Librarian speaks on searching tips such as Boolean operators, etc.
- Students demonstrate how to go backward, use hyperlinks, deal with pop-up windows, and open new windows.
- Librarian speaks on a few tips and safety tricks: how to save favorites, how to close a window or stop a download that is a security threat, and basics on junk/spam websites and how to recognize them early before you link to them.
- Students demonstrate how to navigate the library's website, giving particular attention to searching the catalog and using the seniors department website.

Additional Tools and Ideas:

How is this different from a library-wide workshop? First, speed—take things slowly and leave room for lots of questions—and secondly, depth. This single workshop doesn't need to be crammed to the gills with too much information. Keep things simple and lighthearted.

Older adults all have different reasons and goals for using the Internet. Find out these reasons and goals before class starts and see if you can incorporate them. Perhaps, during workshop time, you may have a chance to print off a specialized list of information links for a patron or find him or her a flier for an upcoming program.

Another idea is to have a theme to the whole workshop or a goal that the group comes up with before starting—a shared interest or even something silly, like the worst food recipes containing curry. That way the entire workshop is geared to one goal. Patrons/teen companions can report on how they did and compare findings and tips.

Promotion:

Have in-house resources available for browsing one month before program.

Have all approved Internet resources linked to a page called "Surfing for Seniors" on the senior department website.

Connectivity Goals:

Dare we go into a lengthy spiel about the benefits of connectivity that the Internet provides? Beyond the obvious of connecting seniors to distant people, places, and things, learning basic technology skills creates a working vocabulary that is becoming increasingly necessary to understand current news, teens, working adults, and the changing pace of life.

* * *

Program: Online Entertainment

Umbrella: Tech Bytes

Learning Goals:

1. Learn about online entertainment that comes to you: blog reader, email lists, etc.
2. Discover In-browser entertainment including movies and games
3. Find out tips on safety for downloadable entertainment

Potential Guests:

- Intergenerational: teen Internet guru

Setup Tips and Materials:

You will need the following:

1. Access to computers
2. A projector to show a computer screen
3. Handouts with instructions

In-House Resources and Technology:

Websites for Movies, TV, and Video

- YouTube: http://www.youtube.com
- Netflix (monthly fee): www.netflix.com
- TV networks websites: Often provide full episodes of their programming, but will include lengthy interruptions for commercials. See the following examples:
  - *Storycorps*: http://storycorps.org/
  - PBS, *Antiques Road Show* (watch free episodes online): http://www.pbs.org/wgbh/roadshow/video
- Rotten Tomatoes: http://www.rottentomatoes.com
  Read movie reviews and create your own reviews!

Websites for Blog Following

- Google Reader: http://www.google.com/reader
  Search for, add, and follow blogs on topics that interest you!
- Blog Express: http://www.snapfiles.com/get/blogexpress.html
- Bloglines Reader: http://www.bloglines.com

Websites for Free Online Games

- 50 Something Games:http://www.50something.us/modules.php?name=Games
  Free to sign up for and use, but must be a member to access the free games.
- AARP Games: http://games.aarp.org
- Pogo: http://www.pogo.com/all-games

- Bing: http://www.bing.com/entertainment/games
- MSN: http://zone.msn.com/en-us/home
- Games.com: http://www.games.com
- Download.cnet.com: http://cnet.co/ky9bq1
- Thinks: http://thinks.com
- Great Bridge Links: http://greatbridgelinks.com
- Memory Improvement Tips -Games: http://www.memory-improvement-tips.com/free-memory-improvement.html
- Boatload Puzzles: http://www.boatloadpuzzles.com/playcrossword
- Games for the Brain: http://www.gamesforthebrain.com
- Crossword Puzzles: http://www.crossword-puzzles.co.uk
- Free Rice (earn money for charity while stimulating your brain with vocabulary words): http://www.freerice.com
- *Guardian News* Sudoku: http://www.guardian.co.uk/lifeandstyle/series/sudoku
- Sudoku Shack (a website for Sudoku games): http://www.soduko.org/

Sample Presentation:

- Librarian introduces the computer as a tool for entertainment and talks about the free games that already come with many computers.
- Librarian discusses blogs/readers and email lists. Patrons learn about how to use a blog reader program (Google Reader) to search for blogs, add their addresses, and follow a hobby. They can also learn to sign up for email lists.
- Speaker: Teen guru talks about in-browser gaming and video, defines what that means, and shows off favorite sites for watching content, like YouTube, or a game they play online. Even if the teens' interests are different than the older patrons', their enthusiasm is what will sell.
- Librarian discusses downloading entertainment programs with a focus on safety. For example, Netflix might make a patron download a program, which is just fine, but a random website that offers free games might require the same thing, which is not advisable, unless it's a trusted website. Also include a discussion on programs that cost money.
- Librarian presents collected and suggested websites for free video and gaming and talks about games that interact with other real people versus just playing against the computer. Include how to access them from the senior's website.

Additional Tools and Ideas:

If you find a game that is really popular such as online Scrabble, conduct a tournament with prizes.

Promotion:

Have in-house resources available for browsing one month before program.

Have all approved Internet resources linked to a page called "Online Entertainment" on the senior department website.

If you decide to conduct a game tournament, maybe a senior center would like to play the same game. The participants could play right from the center. It could be a city-wide game!

Connectivity Goals:

Learning about online gaming and entertainment can create a vocabulary and skill set that will allow older patrons to better interact with their grandchildren. They can play online games with people from around the world.

They can comment and interact with other viewers of online video. They may even write great reviews of movies to post on http://www.rottentomatoes.com.

* * *

Program: Digital Books and E-Readers

Umbrella: Tech Bytes

Learning Goals:

1. Definition of digital book
2. Learn the pros and cons of digital books
3. Discover how to access digital books via computer
4. Learn about the variety of e-readers available
5. Find out where their library stands on digital books/services available

Potential Guests:

- A college student who loves e-readers

Setup Tips and Materials:

A roundtable format would work the best so patrons can keep the example e-readers near a surface. That way, if you have to pass around borrowed e-readers or even your own personal one, there is less chance for damage if it is dropped.

You will need the following:

1. A projection screen
2. Access to computers
3. Handouts with instructions

A variety of e-readers should be obtained for the program, such as:

- Kindle by Amazon: http://www.amazon.com/kindle
- Nook by Barnes & Noble: http://www.barnesandnoble.com/nook/index.asp
- Sony Reader: http://bit.ly/jviSDs
- Samsung Galaxy Tab: http://www.samsung.com/us/mobile/galaxy-tab

Note: Each e-reader's maker offers free downloads on their website, and new e-readers are being offered all the time. So check for the latest e-readers and what they have to offer.

In-House Resources and Technology:

Websites

- *Wikipedia*
  "Comparison of E-Book Readers": http://en.wikipedia.org/wiki/Comparison_of_e-book_readers
  "E-Book": http://en.wikipedia.org/wiki/E-book
- Project Gutenberg (over 38,000 free books with expired copyrights for download to PC or e-readers; also features audiobooks): http://www.gutenberg.org, http://www.gutenberg.org/browse/categories/1 (audiobooks)
- Find your Libraries Online Library, usually a state-wide collaborative.
  Example: http://pioneer-library.org
- Many Books: http://www.manybooks.net
  Offers free book downloads.

- Adobe Digital Editions: http://www.adobe.com/products/digitaleditions
  Provides free program to read e-books on your computer.
- Online Books: http://onlinebooks.library.upenn.edu
- Inkmesh (compares e-book prices): http://www.inkmesh.com

Videos

- YouTube: Search "e-reader comparisons" to find the latest and greatest.
  Example: http://www.youtube.com/watch?v=1smnU5pRnPU
  Since technology is always changing, search for "how-to" videos on the exact e-readers your library uses, as well as for those you might be using in your presentation.
  Example: Barnes and Noble Nook Color e-Reader Tips and Tricks: http://www.youtube.com/watch?v=DIUk6DbRZSk
- *Eli Neiburger at the LJ/SLJ eBook Summit: Libraries Are Screwed*
  http://www.youtube.com/watch?v=KqAwj5ssU2c (Part 1)
  http://www.youtube.com/watch?v=bd0lIKVstJg (Part 2)
- *The Story of the Digital Book*: http://www.youtube.com/watch?v=qK9tyxufw_s
- The Future of Book Publishing: New York Public Library Roundtable 2011:
  Harlequin Exec Says E-Books Will Not Replace P-Books: http://www.youtube.com/watch?v=ErE0zjzEQs0
  Author Melinda Roberts Says E-Books Will Not Replace P-Books: http://www.youtube.com/watch?v=P46B2fHIesU

Sample Presentation:

- Librarian introduces the topic of digital books and e-readers.
- Librarian discusses the pros and cons of digital content, as well as his or her stance on the subject.
- Librarian presents how to access books (free ideally) via computer and shows off what the library has to offer in this regard. Any special features like read aloud or large print should be demonstrated.
- Speaker: Guest college students bring in and talk about their Kindle (or other) e-reader and how it has been useful to them.
- Librarian presents a variety of e-readers and demonstrates how to access content. Hopefully the library has some for checkout or in-library use.
- Librarian concludes with a discussion on the future of e-readers and maybe his or her own opinion of the role of libraries in the whole debate.

Additional Tools and Ideas:

E-readers are the ultimate prize. Have a contest. Maybe the senior who comes to the most programs throughout the year will win a donated e-reader.

Even if the whole library can't be on board, perhaps seniors can be recipients of a grant or as a group can be used to solicit donations for a check-out program for e-readers. Fill them with free books! It may be the test for gaining funds to buy e-readers for the entire library.

Promotion:

Digital books are great for seniors! E-readers are easy to carry, some have read-aloud features, text size can be adjusted, books can be previewed easily, and costs are coming down. Be sure to play up the benefits and the role of libraries in the digital revolution.

Have in-house resources available for browsing one month before the program.

Have all approved Internet resources linked to a page called "Digital Books and E-Readers" on the senior department website.

Connectivity Goals:

Get seniors on board with your library's stance on the digital revolution. Seniors could be active participants on committees, patron boards, or even letter-writing campaigns.

WELLNESS WATCH SERIES

Today's seniors are living longer than any generation before them. Despite medical advances during the course of their lifetime, a majority of people today are unhealthy. Obesity and diabetes are on the rise. Knowing there are still a lot of years ahead of them, many of today's seniors are taking an active role in the upkeep of their health and medical care. Feeling great is the key to making the most of additional years, now more than ever. Being active, keeping in shape, treating health problems successfully, and eating healthy are all important topics that are gaining in popularity. Older adults want to find out about the latest research, the newest fads, and how to communicate to their doctors effectively. They are finding fun and interesting ways to get in shape, eat healthier, and gain health knowledge.

The library is the perfect partner to foster awareness of these topics due to our wealth of information resources. We are in the ideal situation to help seniors connect to a community that shares their same health care issues, interests, and needs. This can be accomplished through local channels including in-house resources, clubs, activities, and support groups or through technology with blogs, wikis, websites, and forums. Empowering older adults with the tools they will need to find an active voice and participate in their health is a role librarians can undertake proudly.

Partnerships

Partners are essential for this category of programming as they can help link seniors to the local community. An endless supply of speakers can be obtained for free or little cost. Arrange for guest speakers from health departments, area doctors or physicians, authors in the health field, personal trainers, nutritionists, and even tai chi or yoga instructors.

Programs

The following is a list of programs that we have created in full for your use.

- Getting the Scoop on Health Insurance
- Planning for an Environmental or Home Emergency
- Posture: How to Beat the Slouch
- The Food Revolution
- Trendy Nutrition: Gimmicks or Good for You?
- Alternative Medicine: What Can It Offer You?
- Fitness Your Way
- Becoming an Informed Patient
- How to Manage Your Health Care
- How to Thrive during a Hospitalization

Other Suggestions

Creating programming sometimes requires reliance on local resources. Some of our great ideas need extra local flavor that only you can add while other ideas are worth highlighting but don't need a full-length program. These ideas could function as simple links on your website or information displayed on kiosks.

- Common senior woes: Local resources and free available aid
    Diabetes, heart disease, glaucoma, kidney disease, hearing problems, arthritis
- Your health and pollution: How to find out what's in your air and water. Is it affecting your health? What can you do? Provide health tips and details on how to get involved locally to be a voice for change.
- Healthy cooking: Include demos from local chefs (check local ordinances about the legality and liability of preparing and serving food) or have them provide a recipe, talk about their philosophy, promote their restaurant, and give out gift coupons or promote their senior discount.
- Mental health: Local health department or mental health services could provide a speaker to talk about the various modalities and low-cost options; self-help books, meditation, and even diet could be discussed.
- Finding energy and falling asleep: This program could involve natural doctors, health food stores, lots of books, and tons of articles and research.

* * *

Program: Getting the Scoop on Health Insurance

Umbrella: Wellness Watch

Learning Goals:

1. Understanding the health care coverage you currently have
2. Learn how to make the best use of your current coverage
3. Learn options for increasing that coverage

Potential Guests:

- Speaker from the local Medicaid or Medicare office
- A medical biller with tips and money-saving options

Setup Tips and Materials:

Caregivers are going to have a huge interest in this program. Be sure that there is extra seating and plenty of time for questions and answers. We recommend a projector. This will allow a document such as an "Explanation of Benefits" to be presented and explained with ease.

You will need the following:

1. Projector
2. Handouts are a must
3. Examples with explanations are a great tool

In-House Resources and Technology:

Books

Social Security, Medicare, and Government Pensions: Get the Most out of Your Retirement and Medical Benefits by Joseph Matthews Attorney and Dorothy Matthews Berman, ISBN 1413313272.
This book has all the free info available online consolidated into one place for ease of use and help with retirement planning.

Caregiving Simplified/Navigating the Medical Insurance Maze/Best Health Care Products Guide by Laurin Grey, ISBN 0557736595.

Websites

- Medicare: http://www.medicare.gov
  CMS.gov, "Medicare" (here you can find doctors and learn more about your plan): http://www.cms. gov/home/medicare.asp
- Medicare Rights Center (nonprofit): http://www.medicarerights.org
- Medicaid: http://www.medicaid.gov/

Videos

- Caretalk: *Making the Most of Medicare*: http://www.youtube.com/watch?v=weExw8XHZCI
- *Medicare Rights Center*: http://www.youtube.com/user/MedicareRightsCenter

Sample Presentation:

- Introduction: Describe current insurances and how they differ.
- Speaker from local Medicare office presents information about how to use your current account and search for doctors, copays, and benefits, as well as details on when to pay a bill or wait.
- Librarian presents online tools for managing Medicaid and Medicare.
- Speaker: Medical biller explains how to work the system for all it's worth, including how to talk to medical billers to get discounts, payment plans, and better service.
- Librarian presents any additional resources and talks about handouts.

Additional Tools and Ideas:

If there is a local nonprofit or even a few medical billers willing to donate some time, it would be amazing to be able to provide a resource to patrons where they could find help sorting out their current situation and medical bill history.

Promotion:

Have in-house resources available for browsing one month before your program. Contact all local government offices that are part of the presentation and provide your contact with handouts or an email version that they can print. Local senior day centers and senior housing may be willing to put out fliers as well.

Have all approved videos and Internet resources linked to a page called "Insurance and You" or some other fun name on the senior department website. Be sure to include downloadable checklists and forms.

Connectivity Goals:

Help older adults get in touch with local nonprofits that can advocate for them.

* * *

Program: *Planning for an Environmental or Home Emergency*

Umbrella: Wellness Watch

Learning Goals:

1. Learn about preparation for staying safe at home, such as food storage, document safety, prescription meds planning, emergency supplies

2. Learn about preparation for evacuation, such as how to keep your home safe and take only the essentials
3. Learn about preparation for sudden emergencies/disasters including where to go for help, other situations like roadside emergencies, or accidents inside the home

Potential Guests:

- Representative from the local Red Cross or the local environmental disaster planning office
- Representative from the local department of public safety
- Representative from a local emergency supply store
    Note: Ask speakers to focus on free and low-cost options.

Setup Tips and Materials:

Avoid creating panic at all cost. Focus on the disasters that can occur in your local area as well as those that can happen to anyone in their home or car. Include local stories: for example, if a creek flooded locally and the library has some interesting photographs, it could lead into a discussion on home flooding.

You will need the following:

1. Samples of food storage items from a local emergency store that will offer a senior discount or already does
2. Checklists and handouts that include additional resources

In-House Resources and Technology:

Books

Handbook to Practical Disaster Preparedness for the Family by Arthur T. Bradley, ISBN 1453678875.
    This book has detailed information on how to create a disaster preparedness plan for your entire family. It also goes into details about a variety of situations, including sheltering in a vehicle.

Organize for Disaster by Judith Kolberg, ISBN 0966797043.
    This book talks about federal resources available and how to get them and also includes information on disasters caused by terrorists.

Making the Best of Basics: Family Preparedness Handbook by James Talmage Stevens, ISBN 0983046530.
    This book has lots of details about food storage and preparation.

Videos (more are posted every day on YouTube . . . free!)

- *Survival Planning on a Budget* (food storage emphasis): http://www.youtube.com/watch?v=gF8x D64clqQ
- *Emergency Preparedness Video* (this series featuring actress Raven-Symoné might be overly simple but has great information). http://www.youtube.com/watch?v=JNmgAIYPT4U
- *Emergency Preparedness Kit for Your Emergency Survival: Insightful Nana* (includes great ideas, like window signs): http://www.youtube.com/watch?v=oDjnyYcnNGY

Websites

- Ready.gov: http://www.ready.gov
    Includes information listed by disaster and services listed by state. Also provides short videos.
- Red Cross: http://www.redcross.org
    This site is the go-to organization for disasters. It has tons of checklists and a store with approved emergency preparedness supplies.

Sample Presentation:

- Find out specific concerns from the audience. Make sure those items get addressed before the program is over.
- Speaker: Red Cross representative speaks about the services they offer.
- Librarian shows clips from free online videos.
- Speaker: Emergency supply store owner talks about which supplies are most necessary.
- Librarian reads from selected books or online resources, holds a discussion, and provides handouts.
- Share concerns and create solutions. Provide the resources to solve.

Additional Tools and Ideas:

Provide a water filtration demo, show a transportable emergency kit or samples of reconstituted food storage, and pass out any free handouts/items from sponsors or the Red Cross.

Promotion:

Have in-house resources available for browsing one month before program. Line up with a locally sponsored emergency preparedness week to get free advertising.

Have all approved videos and Internet resources linked to a new emergency page on the senior department website. Be sure to include downloadable checklists and forms.

Connectivity Goals:

Put seniors in contact with their local neighborhood senior center. They may have emergency sheltering and additional resources. Encourage resource sharing and tips.

Urge patrons to connect with their neighbors so they can keep track of each other should there be a crisis.

* * *

Program: Posture: How to Beat the Slouch

Umbrella: Wellness Watch

Learning Goals:

1. Learn what defines a slouch
2. Learn about the medical implications. Can you change your posture or do you need to consult a doctor? In older women in particular, osteoporosis or even scoliosis might be a medical issue.
3. Find out what makes for good/natural posture
4. Discover the ideal posture for walking, sitting, or working out
5. Learn about accessory equipment such as standing desks, kneeling chairs, balls, and barefoot shoes

Potential Guests:

- Yoga instructor
- Chiropractor
- Barefoot running enthusiast (or perhaps focus on barefoot walking)
  Note: This is the term for the new trend of those who usually wear minimalist shoes for foot protection; it's not only for running, but walking and standing as well.

In-House Resources and Technology:

You will need the following:

1. Props on hand like kneeling chairs, stability/exercise balls, barefoot shoes like Vibram's Five-Finger Shoes
2. Access to computers
3. A projector to show a computer screen
4. Handouts with instructions

Books

The New Rules of Posture: How to Sit, Stand, and Move in the Modern World by Mary Bond, ISBN 1594771243.
8 Steps to a Pain-Free Back: Natural Posture Solutions for Pain in the Back, Neck, Shoulder, Hip, Knee, and Foot (Remember When It Didn't Hurt) by Esther Gokhale, ISBN 9780979303609.
Barefoot Running Step by Step: Barefoot Ken Bob, the Guru of Shoeless Running, Shares His Personal Technique for Running with More Speed, Less Impact, Fewer Injuries, and More Fun by Roy M. Wallack and Barefoot Ken Bob Saxton, ISBN 9781592334650.
Barefoot Running (Volume 1) by Michael Sandler and Jessica Lee, ISBN 0984382208.
   This book has a special section on seniors.
The New Yoga for Healthy Aging: Living Longer, Living Stronger, and Loving Every Day by Suza Francina, ISBN 9780757305320.
Yoga for Arthritis: The Complete Guide by Loren Fishman and Ellen Saltonstall, ISBN 9780393330588.
Pilates for Fragile Backs: Recovering Strength and Flexibility after Surgery, Injury, or Other Back Problems by Andra Fischgrund Stanton and Ruth Hiatt-Coblentz, ISBN 1572244666.
Working on the Ball: A Simple Guide to Office Fitness by Jane Clapp and Sarah Robichaud, ISBN 9780740756993.

Websites

- ElderGym (Website includes videos):
    Elderly Posture: http://www.eldergym.com/elderly-posture.html
    Correcting Bad Posture: http://www.eldergym.com/correcting-bad-posture.html
- DocStoc, "Exercises for Poor Posture in the Elderly": http://www.docstoc.com/search/exercises-for-poor-posture-in-the-elderly
- Esther Gokhale: https://egwellness.com
    Offers many free hints and tips as well as pictures of bad posture and natural posture.
- Living Barefoot (articles and information about healthy feet): http://www.livingbarefoot.info
- Society for Barefoot Living: http://www.barefooters.org
- Vibram Five Finger Shoes (minimalist shoes): http://www.vibramfivefingers.com

Videos

- *Authors@Google: Esther Gokhale* (offers some posture tips): http://www.youtube.com/watch?v=-yYJ4hEYudE
    Many similar great videos are posted here. Search "Esther Gokhale and the Gokhale Method."
- YouTube: Search "chair yoga for seniors" for more than can be listed!
- *The Barefoot Professor and human foot facts*: http://www.youtube.com/watch?v=y6dn3Tf3spQ
- NPR, "Study: Humans Were Born to Run Barefoot": http://n.pr/mOVZQz
- *10 Daily Posture Exercises for Seniors*: http://www.youtube.com/watch?v=WJspJaFL_l8
- *Stability Ball Workout for Zoomers—Spring Tune Up*: http://www.youtube.com/watch?v=onnUojfa8mY
- *Improve Your Posture with Yoga—Part 1*: http://www.youtube.com/watch?v=DBwsziChV78
    The instructor is a senior as well! Watch all six parts of this series.

- *New York Times,* "Are We Built to Run Barefoot?" by Gretchen Reynolds: http://well.blogs.nytimes. com/2011/06/08/are-we-built-to-run-barefoot

Sample Presentation:

- Librarian presents a slideshow of the slouch.
- Speaker: Chiropractor lectures on the negatives of slouching and describes what type of doctors can check for preexisting spine/back/posture conditions. He or she should also provide tips for good posture.
- Video clip: Show a clip of Esther Gokhale, creator of the Gokhale Method, which promotes better health through better structure: http://www.youtube.com/watch?v=-yYJ4hEYudE
- Speaker: Have a barefoot runner present what it means. This person describes the historic origins of barefoot walking and running, busts myths about the arch-support theory with evidence and opinion, offers advice on how to get started, and explains how it will help posture.
- Speaker: Yoga instructor demonstrates some simple posture-improving techniques and offers advice on how to choose a yoga class.
- Demo: Kneeling chair, posture balls, and barefoot shoes (see if a local shoe shop can provide a selection of sizes and some coupons).

Additional Tools and Ideas:

Make sure to customize this program for seniors—find out what their main concern is. Perhaps it is sitting or something else. Have the program and speakers put a focus on that element.

Make sure to have a disclaimer that older adults should consult their physician before beginning any trial posture-altering regimes.

Barefoot walking/running is becoming a huge phenomenon. It's quite the opposite from the arch-support-is-a-must camp. If you conduct a workshop, guest speakers may be available from the fitness industry as well as from local shoe stores to present minimalist-style shoes.

A walking club could be formed via the library—in the winter, they could walk at local indoor malls.

Promotion:

Be sure to advertise at the local senior center as well as in senior housing.

Find out beforehand what nearby yoga centers have to offer as far as low-impact classes, core-strengthening classes, senior-only classes, and discounts.

Have in-house resources available for browsing one month before program.

Have all approved Internet resources linked to a page called "Posture: How to Beat the Slouch" on the senior department website.

Connectivity Goals:

This computer age has created a whole lot of slouchers. Create intergenerational ties by combining with the teen group.

* * *

Program: The Food Revolution

Umbrella: Wellness Watch

Learning Goals:

1. Find out more about Organic food: Is it really necessary? What are heirloom vegetables?
2. Discover the Slow Food movement
3. Learn about local food, farmers markets, and CSAs (community supported agriculture)

4. Find out about GMOs and food additives
5. Find out about the chemicals used in food production (like the infamous "pink slime") and beauty products

Potential Guests:

- Representative from a local health food store
- Representative from a local alternative medicine store
- Representative from a local organic farm—produce or meat
- Farmer's market guru, organizer, seller, or consumer
- Restaurant owner or chef who uses the Slow Food methodology

Setup Tips and Materials:

In a way, the Slow Food and organic movement is getting back to the farmer roots of older patrons and the hippy roots of boomer patrons. Access that. Remind them that this isn't a new fad but rather a revolutionary movement to take back our roots and our health.

Attend a local farmers market and try to drum up some free samples and speakers. Notice the best parking or access routes and the location of restrooms.

You will need the following:

Access to computers
A projector to show a computer screen
Handouts with maps, lists, hints, and tips
Food samples

In-House Resources and Technology:

Books

Slow Food Nation: Why Our Food Should Be Good, Clean, and Fair by Carlo Petrini and Alice Waters, ISBN 0847829456.
Food Politics: How the Food Industry Influences Nutrition, and Health, Revised and Expanded Edition by Marion Nestle, ISBN 9780520254039.
What to Eat by Marion Nestle, ISBN 9780865477384.
The Organic Food Shopper's Guide by Jeff Cox, IBSN 0470174870.
To Buy or Not to Buy Organic: What You Need to Know to Choose the Healthiest, Safest, Most Earth-Friendly Food by Cindy Burke, ISBN 1569242682.
Organic Manifesto: How Organic Food Can Heal Our Planet, Feed the World, and Keep Us Safe by Maria Rodale, ISBN 9781609611361.
Food, Inc.: Mendel to Monsanto—The Promises and Perils of the Biotech Harvest by Peter Pringle, ISBN 074326763X.
The Omnivore's Dilemma: A Natural History of Four Meals by Michael Pollan, ISBN 9780143038580.
An A–Z Guide to Food Additives: Never Eat What You Can't Pronounce by Deanna M Minic, ISBN 1573244031.
The Hundred-Year Lie: How to Protect Yourself from the Chemicals That Are Destroying Your Health by Randall Fitzgerald, ISBN 9780452288393.
The Fluoride Deception by Christopher Bryson, ISBN 1583227008.
The GMO Trilogy and *Seeds of Deception* by Jeffrey M. Smith, ISBN 9780972966535.

Websites

- Environmental Working Group
  EWG's 2011 Shopper's Guide to Pesticides in Produce: http://www.ewg.org/foodnews/list/
  Skin Deep Cosmetics Database: http://www.ewg.org/skindeep
  A comprehensive database of beauty products rated for safety based on toxic ingredient content.

- Consumers Union, "Organic Foods": http://www.consumersunion.org/pub/f/foodorganic/index.html
    This site offers many articles about organic food.
- LocalHarvest, "Community Supported Agriculture": http://www.localharvest.org/csa
- Mayo Clinic, "Organic Foods: Are They Safer? More Nutritious?": http://www.mayoclinic.com/health/organic-food/NU00255
- USDA, "Food Labeling: Organic Foods": http://1.usa.gov/7JhWaS
- Eat Wild: http://www.eatwild.com,
    Provides links to locally raised wild and grass-fed meat and includes lots of articles.
- Africa Centre for Holistic Management: http://achmonline.squarespace.com/learning-site
    Holistic land management (how free-range cattle can reverse desertification)
    This blog posting from Primal Wisdom, called Earth Medicine: Operation Hope, illustrates the concept nicely: http://donmatesz.blogspot.com/2011/03/operation-hope-meat-is-medicine-for.html

Videos

- *Why Is Organic Food More Expensive*: http://www.youtube.com/watch?v=gTxivVaqpcQ
- Nutrition by Natalie videos (See *Why Organic Food* part 1 and part 2): http://www.nutritionbynatalie.com/videos_nutritionbasics.htm
- *How to Buy Organic Produce—Organic Foods*: http://www.youtube.com/watch?v=AqRyDip3X38
- *How to Choose Organic Skin and Beauty Products*: http://www.youtube.com/watch?v=hu83Q17yQZg
- *Dangers of Food Additives & Preservatives Advances Nutrition*: http://www.youtube.com/watch?v=Kyvs_WnyT1c
- *Truth about Food Additives? Austin Nutrition*: http://www.youtube.com/watch?v=57uyHcnv6Ss
- *The Health Dangers of Genetically Modified Foods* (series by Jeffery Smith): http://www.youtube.com/watch?v=94d-KVorSHM
- *GMO: Are We Playing God? (C0nc0rdance)*: http://www.youtube.com/watch?v=yzTECVk8tVU
- *What Is the Slow Food Movement by the University of Maine?*: http://www.youtube.com/watch?v=pHVUX13G1h0
- *Smart Shopping at Farmers Markets*: http://www.youtube.com/watch?v=rWznDS-kdHE

Movies

- Movie: *The Future of Food* (2005) directed by Deborah Koons Garcia
- Movie: *Deconstructing Supper* (2002) directed by Marianne Kaplan
- TV show *PBS: To Market to Market to Buy a Fat Pig* (2007)

Sample Presentation:

- Librarian introduces the history of food production and explains how it has changed in the past 100 years, such as through increased use of herbicides, pesticides, and fungicides; depletion of natural minerals in the soil; the decline of healthy free-range cattle for stockyard-raised cattle, etc.
- Speaker: Two representatives from a local Whole Foods/Trader Joe's present information on organic food. One is a produce manager who provides a list of the best foods to buy organic and the ones you don't need to worry about. The second speaker is a butcher who describes the various different terminologies used—organic, free range, grass fed, natural, etc.—and what they mean to the consumer.
- Librarian introduces information about food and chemical additives such as artificial sweeteners, carrageen, BPA in plastic and cans, fluoride in drinking water, and those found in beauty products (i.e., sodium lauryl sulfate).
- Speaker: Local chef introduces the Slow Food movement and what it means to his or her restaurant.

- Speaker: Local pig farmer, who has a booth at the local farmers market, talks about how his or her farm raises animals and how that affects the quality of the meat and the local environment.
- Librarian presents maps and tips and handouts for accessing local organic food from the farmers market to local CSAs.

Additional Tools and Ideas:

If you have someone willing to take charge, a group of interested patrons could meet at a local parking area and all go the farmers market together on a set day or time.

CSAs often have designated pickup times and spots for their produce or meats. This may not work for many seniors. Find out if a local CSA will accommodate senior patrons with home delivery.

This entire program works very well with a library vegetable garden initiative, so start one and promote it!

Check out this library's urban garden: *New York Times*, City Room blog, "At This Library: Check Out the Tomatoes," http://cityroom.blogs.nytimes.com/2011/08/16/at-this-library-check-out-the-tomatoes.

Promotion:

Advertise at all local grocery stores and local doctors offices that support healthy eating, including holistic doctors and chiropractic offices.

Have in-house resources available for browsing one month before program.

Have all approved Internet resources linked to a page called "The Food Revolution" on the senior website.

Connectivity Goals:

The Slow Food movement is all about community. Find out where there are local community gardens and how older adults can get involved.

* * *

Program: Trendy Nutrition—Gimmicks or Good for You?

Umbrella: Wellness Watch

Learning Goals:

1. Learn about current diet/lifestyle fads
   Suggestions: Atkins, low-carb/high-fat (a.k.a. Paleo), Mediterranean diet, etc.
2. Find out the current buzzwords, such as superfoods and bad-for-you foods
   Suggestions: pomegranate, acai, wheatgrass, probiotics, sugar controversy, and any other current trends in the media
3. Discover how to cut through the hype

Potential Guests:

- Local nutritionist
- Representative from local health medicine store
- Naturopathic doctor
- Someone following a diet like Atkins or the Mediterranean diet or a lifestyle diet like Paleo or Primal

Setup Tips and Materials:

Since this is really a fact program that promotes fact-finding and research, make sure that access to computers is available so patrons can continue research on their own.

You will need the following:

1. A projector to show a computer screen
2. Handouts

In-House Resources and Technology:

Books

Why We Get Fat by Gary Taubes, ISBN 9780307272706 (low-carb/high-fat).

Wheat Belly by William Davis, ISBN 1609611543 (wheat-free).

The Primal Blueprint: Reprogram Your Genes for Effortless Weight Loss, Vibrant Health, and Boundless Energy by Mark Sisson, ISBN 9780982207703 (Primal lifestyle).

Everyday Paleo by Sarah Fragoso, ISBN 098256581X (Paleo lifestyle).

The Vegetarian Myth: Food, Justice, and Sustainability by Lierre Keith, ISBN 9781604860801 (antivegetarian, eco-sustainability).

Superfoods for Dummies by Brent Agin and Shereen Jegtvig, ISBN 9780470445396.

Superfoods: The Food and Medicine of the Future by David Wolfe, ISBN 9781556437762.

The Mediterranean Diet by Marissa Cloutier, ISBN 0060578785.

Eat, Drink, and Be Healthy: The Harvard Medical School Guide to Healthy Eating by Walter C. Willett, ISBN 0743266420.

Nutrition and Physical Degeneration by Weston A. Price, ISBN 0916764206.

Also include any trendy diet recipe books you have on the shelves already!

Websites

- *New York Times*, "Foods with Benefits, or So They Say": http://www.nytimes.com/2011/05/15/business/ 15food.html?pagewanted=1&_r=1
- Information Is Beautiful, "Snake Oil? Scientific Evidence for Popular Health Supplements": http://www. informationisbeautiful.net/play/snake-oil-supplements
- *New York Times*, "Is Sugar Toxic?" by Gary Taubes: http://nyti.ms/hqckbq
- *The Diet Doctor* (a Swedish doctor who promotes low-carb/high-fat): http://www.dietdoctor.com/lchf
- *Health News Reviews*: http://www.healthnewsreview.org/blog
- *Supplement Secrets Exposed*: http://www.powersupplements.com/blog
    Posting on what makes a superfood popular: http://www.powersupplements.com/blog/480/super foods-oprah
- *Medical News Today*, "Nutrition/Diet News": http://www.medicalnewstoday.com/sections/nutrition-diet
- WebMD: http://www.webmd.com/default.htm
    Search "superfoods" for the latest articles and buzz.

Videos

- *Sugar: The Bitter Truth* by Robert H. Lustig, MD, UCSF professor of pediatrics in the Division of Endocrinology. http://www.youtube.com/watch?v=dBnniua6-oM&ob=av3e
- *Loren Cordain–Origins and Evolution of the Western Diet: Health Implications for the 21st Century* (low-carb, low-fat): http://www.youtube.com/watch?v=5dw1MuD9EP4
- *Fathead the Movie* (2009) directed by Tom Naughton: http://www.hulu.com/watch/196879/fat-head
- Nutrition by Natalie videos (see section on superfoods): http://www.nutritionbynatalie.com/videos.htm
- *Diet Leaders Art DeVany and Robb Wolf on* Nightline *3-1-11*: http://www.youtube.com/watch?v=LoE2X1_ KdOU
- *Gary Taubes on Nightline: Carbohydrates Make You Fat, and Perhaps Sick 9/27/2007*: http://www.you tube.com/watch?v=vnwPSu7B2pM
- *The Truth about Acai Berry: A Real Cure? or A Marketing Scam?*: http://www.youtube.com/watch?v= EiU0rmrFLyE
    There are many videos like this. Pick a superfood of choice and do a search!

Sample Presentation:

- Librarian introduces the idea of consumer empowerment.
- Librarian provides an overview of trendy diets, research, and food.
- Speaker: Naturopathic doctor discusses how he or she incorporates superfoods and keeps up with the latest trends and discusses reasons one may choose to use them. This speaker should cover how to talk to your doctor about a trend you are interested in.
- Librarian discusses how to use library databases and how to choose online sources for accuracy via a sample mini–research project on a group-decided buzzword or superfood (like Omega 3 or pomegranates). Does a website promote a product that they sell, thus reducing the validity of their claims? Is the claim backed up by research?
- Speaker: Library employee on Atkins diet talks about how her or she decided to take up that way of eating. Did he or she do research first or talk to the doctor? Is the speaker monitoring his or her health along with their weight loss?
- Librarian offers ways to find out more: how to join a forum or follow blogs and newsfeeds on health topics.

Additional Tools and Ideas:

Make sure to have a disclaimer that seniors should consult their physician before making any dietary changes.

If there is enough interest in these topics, they can be broken down into short seminars like "The Atkins Diet," "The Low-Carb/High-Fat Diet," "Superfoods from South America," or even "Teas of the World."

Promotion:

Advertise at all local grocery stores and local doctors offices that support healthy eating, including holistic doctors and chiropractic offices.

Have in-house resources available for browsing one month before program.

Have all approved Internet resources linked to a page called "Trendy Nutrition" on the senior department website.

Connectivity Goals:

Senior patrons may have health woes or may want to join an online nutrition community to find out more information. Make sure they know what forum-style websites are and how to join and use them.

* * *

Program: Alternative Medicine—What Can It Offer You?

Umbrella: Wellness Watch

Learning Goals:

1. Find out what makes a medicine alternative
2. Discover what are the most common and accepted forms of alternative medicine
3. Learn how to find out more about a practitioner
4. Learn how to decide if it is right for you (explore research techniques)

Potential Guests:

- Chinese medicine/acupuncture practitioner
- Naturopathic medicine doctor/osteopathic doctor
- Chiropractor

- Someone who has tried alternative therapies
- Researcher, professor, or student of natural medicine

Setup Tips and Materials:

You will need the following:

1. Display area for a demonstration for acupuncture or other practices
2. Access to computers
3. A projector to show a computer screen
4. Handouts

In-House Resources and Technology:

Books

Trick or Treatment: The Undeniable Facts about Alternative Medicine by Edzard Ernst and Simon Singh, ISBN 9780393337785.
Snake Oil Science: The Truth about Complementary and Alternative Medicine by R. Barker Bausell, ISBN 9780195383423.
Alternative Medicine: The Definitive Guide edited by John W. Anderson and Larry Trivieri, ISBN 9781587611414.
Mayo Clinic Book of Alternative Medicine: The New Approach to Using the Best of Natural Therapies and Conventional Medicine by Mayo Clinic, ISBN 1933405929.
Natural Health, Natural Medicine: The Complete Guide to Wellness and Self-Care for Optimum Health by Andrew Weil, ISBN 9780618479030.
Encyclopedia of Natural Medicine, Revised Second Edition by Michael Murray and Joseph Pizzorno, ISBN 9780761511571.
Encyclopedia of Nutritional Supplements: The Essential Guide for Improving Your Health Naturally by Michael T. Murray, ISBN 0761504109.
Acupuncture for Everyone: What It Is, Why It Works, and How It Can Help You by Dr. Ruth Kidson, ISBN 0892818999.
Patient's Guide to Chinese Medicine: Dr. Shen's Handbook of Herbs and Acupuncture by Joel Harvey Schreck, ISBN 9780980175806.
The Gerson Therapy: The Proven Nutritional Program for Cancer and Other Illnesses by Charlotte Gerson and D.P.M. Morton Walker, ISBN 1575666286.

Websites

- *Wikipedia*, definitions
  "Doctor of Osteopathic Medicine": http://en.wikipedia.org/wiki/Doctor_of_Osteopathic_Medicine
  "Doctor of Naturopathic Medicine": http://en.wikipedia.org/wiki/Naturopathic_doctor
  "Ayurvedic Medicine": http://en.wikipedia.org/wiki/Ayurveda
  "Traditional Chinese Medicine": http://en.wikipedia.org/wiki/Traditional_Chinese_medicine
  "Acupuncture": http://en.wikipedia.org/wiki/Acupuncture
  "Chiropractic": http://en.wikipedia.org/wiki/Chiropractic
- National Center for Complementary and Alternative Medicine: http://nccam.nih.gov
  Provides research and articles on health topics.
- Craig Hospital, "Understanding Those Medical and Research Articles": http://www.craighospital.org/SCI/METS/articles.asp
- Natural Herbs Guide: http://www.naturalherbsguide.com
- Herb Research Foundation: http://www.herbs.org/herbnews
- Federation of Chiropractic Licensing Boards: http://bit.ly/j2Zmyi
  Provides a way to check on a chiropractor.

- Quackwatch (articles on alternative medicine): http://www.quackwatch.org
- Natural Medicines Comprehensive Database: http://bit.ly/j7oydx
    This site offers a paid subscription to a database for natural medicine. Consumers can subscribe on their own, or the library may choose to add it to their collection.

Videos

- *Introduction to Acupuncture—CMS*: http://www.youtube.com/watch?v=wXgVz4ZqAxo
- YouTube Channel for user C0nc0rdance, called Real Science, features a entire series of de-bunking videos:
    Natural Cures: http://www.youtube.com/watch?v=r3yzXXPeLo0
    Chiropractic vs. Science Based Medicine (2 parts): *Part 1*: http://www.youtube.com/watch?v=b_bNeS nYTmA and *Part 2*: http://www.youtube.com/watch?v=2NBxShj_MEg
    Acupuncture: http://www.youtube.com/watch?v=pp5eiHUdwb4
    What Is a California Licensed Naturopathic Doctor?: http://www.youtube.com/watch?v=Iyj3jbthpWg
- OhioHealth Representative Talks about What a DO, or Doctor of Osteopathic Medicine Is: http://www.youtube.com/watch?v=6Ll48a2EJqQ
- *Intro to Chiropractic Care*: http://www.youtube.com/watch?v=7B1JJFNUvUs
- *Chiropractic Adjustment*: http://www.youtube.com/watch?v=vXsYPdfcXDU
- *Difference between Medical and Chiropractic Doctors*: http://www.youtube.com/watch?v=opyztV7TkoA
- *UC Television: Complementary and Alternative Medicine*: Ayurvedic Medicine: http://www.youtube.com/watch?v=iTOJ8c__rk8

Sample Presentation:

- Librarian defines alternative medicine and provides an overview of some popular types of alternative treatment (examples: Ayurvedic, biofeedback, herbal, Chinese medicine, acupuncture).
- Speaker: Local naturopathic doctor presents his or her training, current practice, choices behind the treatments used, and treatments he or she doesn't believe in.
- Speaker and demonstration: Acupuncture or acupressure provider should provide a demonstration.
- Librarian provides basic training on how to keep up with medical data on alternative treatments, debunking, and fraud prevention.
- Speaker: Patron with a current or cured health problem who has tried a few alternative treatments. Did the patron research before he or she tried? What would he or she do differently before trying something else new?
- Librarian provides an overview of the resources the library is providing on this topic.

Additional Tools and Ideas:

Make sure to have a disclaimer that seniors should consult their physician before making any medical changes. Demos are a great way to promote this program.

If there is a natural health fair in your area, contact them to see if they will provide a free demo and senior discounts in exchange for promotion.

Local health food store often have demos on natural health in order to sell products in their store. If you choose to promote this, be sure that you provide education in your program or via handouts on how to be an educated consumer.

Promotion:

Advertise at all local grocery stores and local doctors offices that support healthy eating, including holistic doctors and chiropractic offices.

Have in-house resources available for browsing one month before program.

Have all approved Internet resources linked to a page called "Alternative Medicine" on the senior department website.

Connectivity Goals:

Senior patrons may have health woes or may want to join an online community to find out more information. Make sure they know what forum-style websites are and how to join and use them.

* * *

Program: Fitness Your Way

Umbrella: Wellness Watch

Learning Goals:

1. Learn about the latest trends in fitness
2. Learn how to participate in fitness even with limitations
3. Discover local resources for fitness
4. Learn about injury prevention and safety

Potential Guests:

- A teacher or practitioner of yoga, tai chi, or water aerobics
- A barefoot running aficionado
- An avid local hiker
- A personal trainer

Setup Tips and Materials:

Have an area open for demonstrations. Have sturdy chairs available for any chair yoga or exercise demonstrations.

You will need the following:

1. Access to computers
2. A projector to show a computer screen
3. Handouts

In-House Resources and Technology:

Books

Senior Fitness: The Diet and Exercise Program for Maximum Health and Longevity by Ruth E. Heidrich, ISBN 9781590560747.

Strength Training for Seniors: How to Rewind Your Biological Clock by Michael Fekete, ISBN 9780897934787.

Water Exercise: 78 Safe and Effective Exercises for Fitness and Therapy by Martha White, ISBN 9780873227261

T'ai Chi for Seniors: How to Gain Flexibility, Strength, and Inner Peace by Philip Bonifonte, ISBN 9781564146977.

Bonnie Prudden's After Fifty Fitness Guide by Bonnie Prudden, ISBN 1461031168.

Barefoot Running Step by Step: Barefoot Ken Bob, the Guru of Shoeless Running, Shares His Personal Technique for Running with More Speed, Less Impact, Fewer Injuries, and More Fun by Roy M. Wallack and Barefoot Ken Bob Saxton, ISBN 9781592334650.

Barefoot Running (Volume 1) by Michael Sandler and Jessica Lee, ISBN 0984382208.

   This book has a special section on seniors.

The New Yoga for Healthy Aging: Living Longer, Living Stronger, and Loving Every Day by Suza Francina, ISBN 9780757305320.

Yoga for Arthritis: The Complete Guide by Loren Fishman and Ellen Saltonstall, ISBN 9780393330588.
Pilates for Fragile Backs: Recovering Strength and Flexibility after Surgery, Injury, or Other Back Problems by Andra Fischgrund Stanton and Ruth Hiatt-Coblentz, ISBN 1572244666.
Working on the Ball: A Simple Guide to Office Fitness by Jane Clapp and Sarah Robichaud, ISBN 9780740756993.

Websites

Remember to include links to county and city recreation centers and programs at public parks, links to gyms and classes with senior classes and/or discounts, and links to sites with local walking/hiking trails.

- *Senior Journal* articles on fitness: http://seniorjournal.com/Fitness.htm
  "Patients with Chronic Heart Failure Discover New Quality of Life with Tai Chi Exercise": http://seniorjournal.com/NEWS/Fitness/2011/20110425-PLatientsWithChronicHeart.htm
- AARP articles:
  "9 Best Exercise Tips for Boomers": http://aarp.us/fUPS7U
  "Water Works Aquatic Activity: A Painless Way to Stay Fit": http://aarp.us/jEHGQU
- MSNBC, "Chair Yoga Catching on among Seniors": http://on.msnbc.com/iLnVtw
- Tai Chi Fitness, "Tai Chi Helps Senior Citizens Maintain Mobility": http://taichifitness.info/tai-chi-helps-senior-citizens-maintain-mobility
- Reuters, "These Malls Are Made for Walking": http://reut.rs/fRE4LW
- American Senior Fitness Association, "Fitness Facts, Tips, and Handouts": http://www.seniorfitness.net/sfafit.htm
- National Institute on Aging, "Exercise and Physical Activity: Your Everyday Guide from the National Institute on Aging": http://www.nia.nih.gov/HealthInformation/Publications/ExerciseGuide

Videos

More videos are available than can be listed on fitness for seniors, and more are posted every single day! So search for these keywords: "fitness for seniors," "chair workouts," "balance and seniors," etc.

- *The Barefoot Professor*: http://www.youtube.com/watch?v=pX265LbH16s
- NPR, "Study: Humans Were Born to Run Barefoot": http://n.pr/mOVZQz
- *Comparison of Minimalist Running Shoes vs. Standard Running Shoes*: http://www.youtube.com/watch?v=FdRoyEDTbFI
- *10 Daily Posture Exercises for Seniors*: http://www.youtube.com/watch?v=WJspJaFL_18
- *Stability Ball Workout for Zoomers—Spring Tune Up* http://www.youtube.com/watch?v=onnUojfa8mY
- *Senior Fitness—Exercises for the Over 60's* (three-part series taught by a 95-year-old):
  Part 1: http://www.youtube.com/watch?v=6m0KjKeF_hY
  Part 2: http://www.youtube.com/watch?v=gfN8C_9aEDo
  Part 3: http://www.youtube.com/watch?v=vOBAe1iF1kE
- *Movements for Balance and Strength—Balance Challenge*: http://www.youtube.com/watch?v=bGGMG4FcwAE
  See all of her short videos, too! (Username: Balance Basics)
- *Fitness Hour of Power—With Kevin*: http://www.youtube.com/watch?v=zWHBcVS3QpA
- *Tai Chi in the Park*: http://www.youtube.com/watch?v=zpQhS_RiQb8
- *Why Yoga?*: http://www.youtube.com/watch?v=ABxRB4cWUeY
- *Yoga for Beginners* (lots of yoga videos by Esther Ekhart, her username is yogatic): http://www.youtube.com/watch?v=H3vLZqPZxZE
- *Yoga for the New Beginner*: http://www.youtube.com/watch?v=C4DLX0Au9WE
- Senior Fitness Exercises: Senior Health and Fitness Exercise Safety Tips: http://www.youtube.com/watch?v=C_YQdLYA4xA

- Everybody Walk, "Mall Walking a Year-Round Solution": http://everybodywalk.org/component/content/article/92-films-community/346-mall-waling-a-year-round-solution.html
- eHow, "Senior Fitness Exercises": http://www.ehow.com/videos-on_2121_senior-fitness-exercises.html

Sample Presentation:

- Librarian introduces the various types of fitness: low impact, high impact, fitness with limitations, and chair workouts; include tai chi, yoga, swim aerobics, ballroom dancing, hiking, walking, and your favorites.
- Speaker: Local hiker presents easy-to-access and safe walking trails in the area, or librarian provides an overview of local walking parks.
- Speaker: Local personal trainer presents safety tips for senior patrons to have a safe workout and demos some easy at-home exercises. Librarian offers additional safety tips, especially for personal safety (pepper spray, not wearing headphones, best times of day, what to bring: water, medications, phone).
- Speaker: Local tai chi teacher provides an overview of tai chi—history, benefits, and where classes are taught—and a demonstration.
- Librarian provides an overview of the resources the library provides, including fitness DVDs, and goes over the local low-cost options, senior discount fitness activities (examples: classes at recreation or senior centers, classes at gyms or studios with a discount, park recreation, malls that open early for walkers, and local walking trails).

Additional Tools and Ideas:

Make sure to have a disclaimer that seniors should consult their physician before making any physical fitness changes.

Barefoot walking is the latest and hottest trend! In this case, *barefoot* actually means the use of minimalist shoes. It flies in the face of the traditional arch-support necessity! If your patrons are progressive, this would be a great program demo. Find a local shoe store willing to a do a presentation on minimalist shoes.

Promotion:

Have in-house resources available for browsing one month before program.

Have all approved Internet resources linked to a page called "Fitness Your Way" on the senior website.

Connectivity Goals:

Although accommodating fitness at home, chair workouts, and fitness DVDs are great ways to stay healthy, fitness is also a great way to connect seniors to their community. Sometimes that very lack of community acts as a roadblock to fitness. Work with local senior centers and gyms to help older adults meet up so they can work out together, perhaps as a walking club or a seniors-only yoga class at the local community center. Or it can be as simple as a ride-share signup for water aerobics.

* * *

Program: Becoming an Informed Patient

Umbrella: Wellness Watch

Learning Goals:

1. Learn about resources available in the library
2. Learn how to discover community resources
3. Learn how to find online resources
4. Discover ways to manage all that information
5. Find out how to talk to your doctor about your findings

Potential Guests:

- A guest speaker who has improved his or her health through education
- A health care provider and/or representative from the local health department

Setup Tips and Materials:

You will need the following:

1. Access to computers
2. A projector to show a computer screen
3. Handouts

In-House Resources and Technology:

Books

The Web-Savvy Patient: An Insider's Guide to Navigating the Internet when Facing Medical Crisis by Andrew Schorr, ISBN 1456324993.

The Empowered Patient: How to Get the Right Diagnosis, Buy the Cheapest Drugs, Beat Your Insurance Company, and Get the Best Medical Care Every Time by Elizabeth S. Cohen, ISBN 0345513746.

You Bet Your Life! The 10 Mistakes Every Patient Makes: How to Fix Them to Get the Healthcare You Deserve by Trisha Torrey, ISBN 9781934938881.

The Empowered Patient: Hundreds of Life-Saving Facts, Action Steps, and Strategies You Need to Know by Dr. Julia A. Hallisy, ISBN 0615177913.

Laugh, Sing, and Eat Like a Pig: How an Empowered Patient Beat Stage IV Cancer (And What Healthcare Can Learn from It) by Dave deBronkart, ISBN 0981650430.

YOU: The Smart Patient: An Insider's Handbook for Getting the Best Treatment by Michael F. Roizen and Mehmet C. Oz, ISBN 0743293010.

Websites

- National Institutes of Health (NIH) Senior Health: http://nihseniorhealth.gov
  Provides descriptions and information on a number of health topics.
- NIH Medline Plus: http://www.nlm.nih.gov/medlineplus
  Contains links to health information, research, and articles, including supplements and drug information.
- NIH Clinical Trials: http://clinicaltrials.gov
  Search for clinical trials by condition or on certain drugs.
- The Empowered Patient: http://www.theempoweredpatient.com/resources.html
  Offers a huge list of resources for the patient that wants to know more.
- *Medical News Today,* "Seniors News and Aging News": http://www.medicalnewstoday.com/sections/seniors
  Medical news updated daily that includes articles, research, forums, and videos.
- Internet-Informed Patient Symposium: http://www.iip-symposium.info
  Click on their "background reading" tab for a number of articles on informed patients.
- University of Texas System, "Tips for Savvy Medical Web Surfing": http://www.utsystem.edu/benefits/newsletter/articles/08apr_wel.htm
- *Huffington Post,* "Are You an Informed Patient?": http://huff.to/5MSCDI
- WebMD: http://www.webmd.com
  Provides descriptions and information on a number of health topics.
- WebMD Community: http://exchanges.webmd.com/default.htm
  WebMD offers forum groups for many health problems.
- Fat Head, "Speech: Science for Smart People" by Tom Naughton: http://www.fathead-movie.com/index.php/2011/05/12/speech-science-for-smart-people/
  This is a speech on how to intelligently read research (using low-carb examples).

- DocFinder: http://www.docboard.org/docfinder.html
  Find your state's medical board to verify a physician is licensed.
- CNN, "Empowered Patient" series: http://www.cnn.com/SPECIALS/empowered.patient/?iref=allsearch
  This series features a variety of stories on a number of health topics where the patient takes an active role in his or her health care.
  Example: "10 Dumb Things You Do at the Doc's Office": http://www.cnn.com/2011/HEALTH/05/26/dumb.doctors.office.ep/
- NC Health Info, "Informed Patient Guide": http://www.nchealthinfo.org/health_topics/health_care/InformedPatientGuide.cfm
- MD Junction: http://www.mdjunction.com
  Provides online support groups for "health challenges."

Videos

- American Public Media, *Makin' Money*: http://bit.ly/czKuqy
  Presents the too-informed patient in the age of WebMD.
- WomensHealthCare, *The Empowered Patient: Communicating with Your Doctor*: http://www.youtube.com/watch?v=EuGh78X2IQw
- KruResearch channel on YouTube: http://www.youtube.com/user/KruResearch
  They are a Think Tank with a focus on empowering patients and offer many videos, for example:
  A Tale of Two e-Patients—Pecha Kucha (presented in Limerick form): http://www.youtube.com/watch?v=9ebdGR3IZp8
  e-Patient Revolution: http://www.youtube.com/watch?v=B7ZrWSmQxcU
- EduAmerica: *How to Become a More Effective e Patient—Part 1 by Dr. Charles Smith*: http://www.youtube.com/watch?v=Jb-yba0M9IE (also see all parts of the series)
- *Insights on the Future of the Patient*: http://www.youtube.com/watch?v=9PQdBs7i90k
  This video is a Creation Healthcare interview of "e-Patient Dave" deBronkart.
- *Jessie Gruman's GoodBehavior!—October 2009—Active, Informed Patients: A New Wild Card*: http://www.youtube.com/watch?v=bR9DHWnfodU

Sample Presentation:

- Librarian introduces the concept of an informed patient and presents library-owned resources, including books and multimedia and the library databases.
- Librarian conducts a mini-workshop on how to do online health research, including the helpful Boolean operators, recommended websites, reliability issues, how to follow a health blog, and how to sign up for a health forum.
- Speaker: One or two persons who have done research that has helped their knowledge or health should present their experiences: How did they get started? What is their favorite resource? Did they talk to their doctor first?
- Speaker: Health care provider discusses how to approach your doctor with your findings. He or she should mention that you should work as a team and discuss how to keep communication from being confrontational.
- Librarian offers tips on how to organize and keep research: when it is better to print information or save it in digital format on your home computer, as well as what to do at a public computer, such as email to home or save to zip drive.

Additional Tools and Ideas:

Make sure to have a disclaimer that seniors should consult their physician before making any changes based on information they discover. Try to avoid any debates about the possibility of patrons changing health care providers if they are not amicable to the newly informed patient.

Offer one-on-one research help for older patrons. Get them started on how to research a health problem with individualized tips and extra help sorting and organizing.

Promotion:

Have in-house resources available for browsing one month before program.

Have all approved Internet resources linked to a page called "Becoming an Informed Patient" on the senior department website.

Connectivity Goals:

Often local support groups as well as online groups exist in your area for every possible health condition. Joining a group like this allows seniors with health issues to find common ground, infuse positive emotions into an often negative situation, and learn a lot. Create a list of all local support groups and update it yearly. Find and create a short list of forums and blogs on the major health issues that come through your library (glaucoma, diabetes, hearing loss, etc).

* * *

Program: How to Manage Your Health Care

Umbrella: Wellness Watch

Learning Goals:

1. Learn how to organize your medical history
2. Discover a variety of options to help organize your current medical quest
3. Find out ways to keep track of your current treatments and medications
4. Learn how to keep bills organized and when to pay
5. Find out additional tips just for caregivers

Potential Guests:

- Organization coach
- Health care provider
- Medical biller

Setup Tips and Materials:

You will need the following:

1. Organizational tools like accordion files, zip drives, an oversize calendar, and medication trays
2. Access to computers
3. A projector to show a computer screen
4. Handouts

In-House Resources and Technology:

Books

The Senior Organizer: Personal, Medical, Legal, Financial by Dorothy Breininger, Lynn Benso, and Debby S. Bitticks, ISBN 0757304893.

Lifetime Medical Organizer: A Simple Guide to Organizing Matters of Life and Health. How-To Instructions and Forms Included by Sandra J. Yorong, ISBN 1434376842.

When Something's Wrong: How to Navigate the World of Health Care by Christina Caskey, ISBN 1608446719.

Taking Charge of Your Own Health: Navigating Your Way through Diagnosis, Treatment, Insurance, and More by Lisa Hall, ISBN 9780736924795.

Navigating the Healthcare Maze: What You Need to Know by Jeff Knott, ISBN 9781932021301.

The Medical Bill Survival Guide: Easy, Effective Strategies for People Experiencing Financial Hardship by Nicholas Newsad, ISBN 9780615352831.

Journal-Style Organizers

My Medical Assistant by Donna B Mccaslin, ISBN 0974970905.
HEALTHMINDER Personal Wellness Journal (a.k.a. MemoryMinder Personal Health Journal) Health Diary and Symptoms Log by F. E. Wilkins, ISBN 9780963796875.
The Wellness Journal: A Personal Health Organizer by Katherine Pierce, ISBN 9780811867214.
My Medical History: A Journal for Keeping Track of Your Health Records by Potter Style, ISBN 0307381854.
Family Caregiver Organizer: A Personal and Medical Journal for Care-Receivers and Their Caregiver(s) by Rebecca Colmer, ISBN 0976546531.

Websites

- Be Ruly, "How to Create a Personal Health Binder to Organize Your Health Records": http://www.beruly.com/?p=5044
- Microsoft Health Vault (a free e-records tracker): http://www.microsoft.com/en-us/healthvault
- PMP Pals' Network, "Organize Your Medical Records for Emergencies": http://bit.ly/kSkE5k
- Suite 101, "How to Organize Personal Medical Records": http://bit.ly/mn8ai3
- Quality Health, "How to Keep Track of Multiple Medications": http://bit.ly/eH1aO8
- Family Doctor.org, "Understanding Your Medical Bills": http://familydoctor.org/online/famdocen/home/pat-advocacy/healthcare/888.html
- Kiplinger, "Save Thousands on Your Medical Bills": http://bit.ly/m1Qten

Videos

- *This System Is Designed to Organize All Your Medical Files*: http://www.youtube.com/watch?v=8Jn4bedWgXQ
- *Medical Records, Why Did You Keep and Organize Them?* http://www.youtube.com/watch?v=AMhnL0MVxzI
- *Bills and Medical Expenses*: http://www.youtube.com/watch?v=J5VbaZ3Nza0
- *Home Organization: How to Organize and File Paper*: http://www.youtube.com/watch?v=pLJGfq2GZoo
- *Keeping Track of Your Medications*: http://www.youtube.com/watch?v=YLsHPlx4188
- *Patient Doctor Communication: Tips for You and the Healthcare Provider to Follow*: http://www.youtube.com/watch?v=0Jmvn84Vz8E
- *Patient Doctor Communication: Legal Documentation and Medical History*: http://www.youtube.com/watch?v=KdvuXB_CgDo

Sample Presentation:

- Librarian introduces the topic with an example of a complicated medical patient (a friend or family member, perhaps). The introduction should focus on the challenges of keeping organized and the dangers of not being organized.
- Speaker: Organization coach presents information basics on how to keep organized with ideas and tips.
- Librarian presents tips and hints garnered from library resources.
- Speaker: Health care professional describes the following: what past and current medical information to bring to an appointment; how to get a copy of all your medical records; and any tips for health care providers (i.e., legal issues).

- Speaker: Medical biller discusses how to tell when to pay and how much, as well as tactics for keeping it all organized and clear.
- Librarian closes with a presentation on library resources.

Additional Tools and Ideas:

Give out free notebooks that can function as health care journals or to take notes in when at the doctors office.

Shoe boxes are a great way to keep track of prescriptions and any changes to dose or pricing. Just make sure to keep them in order by date.

Medical bills can be daunting to read and worrisome to pay if you don't understand them. Find a local non-profit advocacy group or even medical billers willing to donate time to helping seniors understand their medical bills (or advocate for coverage when denied).

Promotion:

Have in-house resources available for browsing one month before program.

Have all approved Internet resources linked to a page called "How to Manage Your Health Care" on the senior department website.

Connectivity Goals:

A patient's doctor appointments, records, bills, and treatments are all very personal; however, seniors can share tips that have worked for them. Make a patron tip section part of the senior website for this program's page. Sharing ideas is a great way to feel connected to others navigating the same maze.

* * *

Program: How to Thrive during a Hospitalization

Umbrella: Wellness Watch

Learning Goals:

1. Learn how to prepare for a planned visit
2. Learn how to be prepared for an emergency visit
3. Discover caregiver tips and guidelines

Potential Guests:

- A medical health care professional
- A former patient who was in the hospital a lot (cancer survivor, etc.)
- A life coach or therapist (for how to stay positive)

Setup Tips and Materials:

You will need the following:

1. Access to computers
2. A projector to show a computer screen
3. Handouts

In-House Resources and Technology:

Books

Hospital Stay Handbook: A Guide to Becoming a Patient Advocate for Your Loved Ones by Jari Holland Buck, ISBN 0738712248.

How to Get Out of the Hospital Alive: A Guide to Patient Power by Sheldon P. Blau and Elaine Fantle Shimberg, ISBN 0028623630.

Critical Conditions: The Essential Hospital Guide to Get Your Loved One Out Alive by Martine Ehrenclou, ISBN 0981524001.

You Bet Your Life! The 10 Mistakes Every Patient Makes—How to Fix Them to Get the Healthcare You Deserve by Trisha Torrey, ISBN 9781934938881.

The Not So Patient Advocate: How to Get the Health Care You Need without Fear or Frustration by Ellen Menard, ISBN 0977819965.

Websites

- Aging Wisely, "Hospital Discharge Checklist for Families" (the hospital discharge process and a for-fee patient advocate): http://www.agingwisely.com/hospital-discharge-checklist-for-families
- CNN, "Nurses Offer Tips for Surviving a Hospital Stay": http://bit.ly/mzK7KP
- Parent Giving, "9 Steps to Surviving a Hospital Stay": http://www.parentgiving.com/elder-care/9-steps-to-surviving-a-hospital-stay
  This article includes rules for the advocating caregiver.
- HelpStartsHere (caregiving articles): http://www.helpstartshere.org/seniors-aging/caregiving
- Find a social worker: http://www.helppro.com/nasw/BasicSearch.aspx
- PBS, This Emotional Life, "When It's Time to Leave: Surviving a Hospital Discharge":
  Part 1—http://to.pbs.org/ajgZh1
  Part 2—http://to.pbs.org/iyBAzm
- Senior Resource Network, "Surviving a Parent's Trip to the Hospital and Beyond: What to Know before You Go": http://bit.ly/miIhhs
- Boca Home Care Services, "Tips to Protect Yourself or an Aging Loved One in the Hospital or Rehab Facility": http://bit.ly/b8vrTt
- *Achoo! Adventures of an Allergist Mommy* blog, "Insider Tips on Surviving a Hospital Stay": http://bit.ly/jzgB8n
- ABC News, "Here's How to Survive Your Hospital Stay": http://abcnews.go.com/Health/WellnessNews/story?id=6999952&page=1

Videos

- *Caregiving Tips: Hospital Stays—Starr Calo-oy*: http://www.youtube.com/watch?v=9WTXP8JF42E
- *Advice from Advocates with Consumers Union's Safe Patient Project* by Consumer Union: http://www.youtube.com/watch?v=H5RdQTWzCoA
- *Surviving the Emergency Room* by Katie Couric: http://www.youtube.com/watch?v=uyVuMDwUT04
- *Patient Advocates* by Johnson and Johnson Health Channel: http://www.youtube.com/watch?v=YY1GJPQ_0uI
- *Top 10 Tips and Tricks for Navigating the Medical Maze* by tiffc73: http://www.youtube.com/watch?v=etEgNrwp7mw

Sample Presentation:

- Librarian introduction: Be prepared, be informed, and be positive.
- Speaker: A former patient tells about their experiences and includes tips.
- Speaker: Nurse from a local ER gives tips on how to thrive in a hospital situation (like having an advocate).
- Speaker: Life coach presents how to stay positive in a difficult situation especially when you are not feeling well.

- Librarian presents any additional tips from in-house resources—especially for caregivers—explains hand-outs, and goes over library resources (and also plugs a program for becoming an informed patient).

Additional Tools and Ideas:

Being in the hospital can feel like it removes an element of control from a person's life. Being informed and organized can return some of that control. Do a mini-demo on how to be an informed patient.

If there is interest, a full caregiver program can be created from elements from many of the programs in the sections—Informed Patient, Managing Your Health Care, Getting the Scoop on Health Insurance.

Promotion:

Have in-house resources available for browsing one month before program.

Have all approved Internet resources linked to a page called "How to Thrive during a Hospitalization" on the senior department website.

Connectivity Goals:

Connect seniors to local services that can help them manage their health care during a hospitalization. There may be local volunteer groups that can visit seniors who lack the support of friends or family during a hospitalization. Or simply provide the local number for contacting a social worker.

RANDOM PROGRAM IDEAS

These are the special kind of programs that just don't fit under a topic umbrella. They could be saved for a special occasion or chosen piecemeal.

Geocaching

This amazing worldwide hobby uses a handheld GPS unit to hunt down urban and rural "caches" of "treasure." Seekers must use GPS coordinates or even game-like hints and tips to find these hidden treasure troves. These caches use sign-in logs and prize exchanges such as coins or DVDs. Finders can connect with people around the world as they exchange their coin for a foreign coin or read the interesting sign-in logs. This fun and exciting hobby is the absolute perfect way to connect with grandchildren. A GPS unit is required to play. This is such a great hobby that we recommend libraries have a set of GPS units on hand for activities in the teen and children's departments. Perhaps a few could be used for technology checkout by seniors.

Knit Tagging

Public art and yarn combine in an activity known by names such as guerilla art, yarn bombing, street knitting, and knit bombing. Those who like to knit have decided it's time they get the artistic credit they deserve. This is done through public displays, sometimes illegally, of knit projects, such as knitting a scarf for a public statue or knitting little hats for parking meters. Of course, this hobby can be done legally by surprising friends and family or simply asking permission of property owners. This new fad has grown in popularity and has sparked a huge surge of interest in knitting. How did we hear about this? From a lifelong knitter turned rogue public art enthusiast, a conservative 75-year-old woman! The library could provide meeting space or have an entire program to introduce the topic along with the basics of wiki creation and use so they could meet on the Web (or free blog or website creation). With a blog, they could showcase their temporary works, which are usually taken away by property owners or stolen. If patrons can check out digital cameras, they can record their art and even have an art show featuring examples and photography.

Finding Your Musical Muse

Music and the library are a great combination. A user-friendly tour of the in-house music collection plus adding an older adult music collection survey can be great starting points. Your programming could also feature an instructional hour of how to access digital music online. It should include how to find music on iTunes to YouTube and beyond, basics of download formats and desktop players, downloading laws, and the best ways to listen to music with iPods. A local music shop could demonstrate what they have in their shops, including any music lessons they have to offer, varieties and formats of music that they sell, or a musical instrument demonstration. Local musical groups, such as local symphony and choruses, could become involved in presentations. This could be as simple as building up to a local musical event, musical theater performance, chorus, or symphony by watching YouTube clips of excerpts and discussing the work, or it could be as complex as a presentation on the history of music featuring clips of singers and musicians that are recreating historical music.

Other Stand-Alone Programming Ideas

- Neighborhood safety: Police officer speaks
- Socializing and dating for the older adult
    Senior Match (dating site for 50+): http://www.seniormatch.com/blogs
    Better Than I Ever Expected blog (sex over 50): http://www.betterthanieverexpected.blogspot.com
    Granny is my Wingman: http://grannyismywingman.com/
    This is a fun website where a "granny" and her granddaughter (the blogger) are both looking for love. They compare notes, have hilarious phone calls, and share their dating advice.
    The Boomer's Guide to Online Dating by Judsen Culbreth, ISBN 9781594862250.
- Alternative lifestyles for the older adult
- Beauty and style for the older adult
    Gorgeous Grandma (beauty and dating tips): http://www.gorgeousgrandma.com
    Style Crone (includes lots of links to similar blogs): http://stylecrone.com
- How to get involved in local politics
- Astrology
- Thrift store fashion
- Thrift store treasures
- Tea time
- Improve your sleep naturally
- Tarot
- Ghosts of _____ (your state, your library). Also, a ghost hunter group could present.
    This might be fun to do in conjunction with a history presentation since ghost sightings often occur in historic buildings and places.

PROGRAM IDEAS THAT NEED LOCAL FLAIR

While each program must be customized to meet the needs of your patrons, this set of program ideas requires extra attention to that facet. From local history to local taste to local events and politics, these foundational ideas will help you build a yearlong monthly series of events.

Urban Garden Series

The outdoor portion will comprise a series of events that can take place in the library arboretum gardens or inside the library. This may be a great excuse to rip up some of that water-guzzling grass and help make the library grounds really green with drip systems and local plants or raised vegetable gardens. Any indoor portions will focus mainly on programs that allow older adults to bring gardening into their homes via learning more about gardening in general, including potted plants, window plants, and patio gardening. Local nurseries and garden centers will be invited as guest speakers and program partners. Local gardening and bird enthusiasts will be guest speakers as well.

Partnerships

Partnerships for this program should include locally owned garden shops, flower shops, community garden organizers, and enthusiasts. Topics for these presentations could be the following:

- How to identify weeds (like local noxious plants)—engage children's department
- Creating a birdhouse from reusable materials
- How to choose and care for indoor plants
- Local birds—what to feed and when (and maybe some suggestions to meet the challenge of keeping squirrels and other animals out of your bird feeders)
- Patio gardening: How to keep those potted plants happy
- Teens join in with planting vegetables in the library garden
- The art of the rose
- The best flowers for hummingbirds, butterflies, and bug repellent
- Creating a birdhouse from reusable materials (like silverware chimes)
- Window gardening: Herbs and more
- Xeriscaping: Local plant life
- Edible plants of your state
- Flower arrangement (can be done near Memorial Day)
- A walk on the wild side: Dangerous plants of your state
- Local wildflowers (highlighting garden tours, clubs, etc.)
- A one-pot salsa garden with a salsa-making demo
- Common garden ailments (pests and fungus are among us!)

Philosophical Forum (A Discussion Group Based on the Socrates Café)

The Socrates Café is an open forum for discussion of a variety of issues and topics first created by Christopher Phillips. Its discussed in his book, *Socrates Café: A Fresh Taste of Philosophy* (ISBN 039332298X) and advocates for active discussion groups. This is a fun and exciting way to discuss hot issues and intellectual topics. Each meeting functions as a sort of round table where participants are divided into small groups. Each meeting has a topic that is open for discussion. These topics can be political, local news, or philosophical in nature. Participants are supposed to question everything and look at each question from all angles in order to understand the topic fully. This is an exploration, rather than a debate. Discussion forums of this nature are designed to improve speaking and listening skills and to keep senior minds active and engaged. As an important component of each meeting is to have a partner group join in. These groups can range from local university students to Friends of the Library to army reserves. These guest presenters can add a fun twist to the meetings. Prior to each meeting, a preparation materials list will be provided, from books to Web articles, enabling seniors to get a broader picture of the issue up for discussion. See more information on the Socrates Café at http://lifeofthemindconsortium.info/SocratesCafe.htm.

Drinks and other snacks are to be potluck and provided. Local bakeries and restaurants should be contacted for donations as they would get free advertisement and promotion.

Discussion topics should reflect local and worldwide events and issues, so you will need to customize the topic choices. Here is a list of some philosophical ideas, along with suggested partner groups.

- White lies? Where is the boundary?
  Middle school honors English class

- Does welfare reward poor behavior?
    High school honors society
- If variety is the spice of life, what can be done about franchising urban sprawl?
    Local university architecture group
- Is it better to give than receive? (Idea by the Socrates Café)
    Local board of a charity group
- Is war ever justified? (Idea by the Socrates Café)
    Community college student body government
- Marriage? A religious right or a civil right? (Idea by the Socrates Café)
    Local
- Should health care only be for crisis incidents, like car insurance? (Idea by the Socrates Café)
    High school health class
- Waste not, want not? (Idea by the Socrates Café)
    Local debate team
- What is the United States' responsibility to the world? (Idea by the Socrates Café)
    Veterans group
- What is the nature of competition?
    Teen book club
- When does prolonging life become suffering? (from the Socrates Café)
    Local nursing students
- Why do people need to believe in a higher power? (from the Socrates Café)
    Local university philosophy club

Blazing Book Club

This seems like a given for any age group at any library. Book clubs are a great way for seniors to keep their minds active and engaged while helping build connections with each other through conversation and fun. Each themed event should include some extras: book lists, decorations, guest speakers, and supplemental information such as the truth behind a fictional stories, more about the author, a discussion about science fiction becoming fact someday, and so on. Coffee and beverages will be provided/allowed.

Additionally, an online component, such as a discussion board, could be initiated if there is enthusiasm for such a venture. This program can also branch out into a senior collection materials advisory board.

Partnerships

While mostly library resources will be used for this club, refreshments are a requirement. While patrons may choose to bring their own, supplementing these by the library and its partners would be appreciated. Local bakeries and restaurants should be contacted for donations as they would be getting free advertisement and promotion.

Ideas

Although your book choices will vary by your patron base and book availability, some suggested genres are the following: autobiographies, Oprah's Book Club, best sellers, books turned into movies, classic novels, historical fiction, local authors, mysteries, and romance.

This is a great way to bring older patrons up to speed on upcoming author visits. You must plan two to three months in advance in order for participants to read a new or more popular novel.

Additionally, include intergenerational programming ties. Once a month, the seniors could join children's storytime to share their favorites growing up. Another month, the teen book club could join the group and show off their favorite books.

Book Talks

Book talks are a wonderful way to incite riots. You heard us, riots! They consist of a librarian or patron choosing a book he or she loved and presenting the following:

1. A dynamic introduction to the main story and characters of the book
2. A passage from the text
3. A positive personal opinion

You might be asking, "Where does the riot part come in?" Well, when you have 10 or 12 now intensely interested patrons all wanting a piece of that one book, a riot is sure to ensue! Better be prepared with additional copies.

Commonly used in school to drum up interest in a new release or upcoming title, these book talks are growing in popularity for seniors. Giving a book talk usually involves presenting about multiple books, totaling up to a 30-minute presentation. Children respond to them like mini-storytimes (but without the librarian giving away the endings), followed by a race to obtain each book even if only to find out what happens in the end, and older adults will respond in the same way.

We suggest you use them in these ways:

- As a program of their own, seasonally or monthly, with program titles like "Tops Picks for Cozy Winter Reading" or "Upcoming Titles for June"
- To fill in cancelled programs
- As a finish to shorter programs, in which case you should only present one or two books

Solicit patrons to be presenters when they rave to you about a favorite book or simply ask for a librarian who is willing to be a presenter. As positive informational sessions, the talks are infinitely more interesting and fun than just reading a book jacket and guessing if it will be a good read. Book talks are an incredible way to "sell" a book while connecting with the reader on a more personal level. A caution: never book talk a book you have not actually read from beginning to end. You may need to answer a question related to the book, and you certainly don't want to be caught in the act of faking a book read!

Sample Book Talks

The Immortal Life of Henrietta Lacks by Rebecca Skloot, Crown Publishers, 2010, 369 pages, hardcover.
Did you know that if you've ever had a simple mole or your appendix removed, your organ or cell sample might be sitting in a lab somewhere for use in scientific research?

Suggested reading: excerpts from the afterword, pp. 318–20, hardcover.

Henrietta Lacks was a poor African American tobacco farmer with cervical cancer in 1950's Baltimore. At a time when scientists were only dabbling in cell research, Henrietta's cancer cells, taken completely without her knowledge by an aspiring cell researcher at Johns Hopkins Hospital, became one of the most important tools used in 20th-century medicine.

Suggested reading: excerpts from chapter 3, "Diagnosis and Treatment," pp. 27–30, hardcover.

Perhaps because of the virulence of Henrietta's cancer, her cells became the first "immortal" human cells grown in culture, something scientists had attempted and failed to do in the past. HeLa cells, as they came to be known, are still bought and sold and used in scientific research today. HeLa cells are still reproducing 60 years later and have been used in research for many scientific advances, including the polio vaccine, cancer research, cloning, and gene mapping. According to the book jacket, if you could pile all the HeLa cells ever grown onto a scale, they'd weigh more than 50 million metric tons, as much as a hundred Empire State Buildings.

Yet the originator of those cells had remained for many years virtually unknown, buried in an unmarked grave. Her name was often misquoted in scientific journals, and Henrietta's family did not learn of the entire issue until more than 20 years after her death. While HeLa cells ushered in a multimillion-dollar industry of selling human biological materials, Henrietta's own family lived in poverty, frequently without health insurance, and like many inner-city poor families, dealt with family members whose drug and violence issues ran them afoul of the law.

Opinion: *The Immortal Life of Henrietta Lacks* is a book provocative of both thought and discussion, bringing to light the controversial issue of using "discarded" human materials in research, without the consent of the contributor; the questionable practice of profiting from those "discarded" materials, also without consent; and the struggle of an uneducated, low-income family to understand and come to terms with a complex ethical medical issue in an increasingly complex society.

The Secret Life of the Grown-up Brain: The Surprising Talents of the Middle-Aged Mind by Barbara Strauch, Viking, 2010, 229 pages.
Beginning with funny and familiar stories about losing our car keys, losing our car, forgetting why we entered a room in the first place, or placing things in the refrigerator that don't belong there, Barbara Strauch starts us off with some light-hearted anecdotes about the aging mind and then goes on to make our hearts even lighter through evidence, both scientific and empirical, that suggests that healthy older brains have a distinct edge over those of our younger counterparts.

Suggested reading: excerpts from chapter 1, "Am I Losing My Mind? Sometimes, but the Gains Beat the Losses," pp. 4–6.

Exploring the concept of wisdom, Strauch offers up examples of how the more complex responses of the older brain actually slow down our reaction time, resulting in less impulsive behaviors and a more thorough exploration of possibilities prior to giving an answer or taking action. Older brains take time to view the big picture. Couple the slower, more thorough thought process with years of experience and voilà, we have wisdom!

Suggested reading: excerpts from chapter 4, "Experience, Judgment, Wisdom," pp. 41–50

Offering tips for keeping our mental faculties functioning at the very best, Strauch suggests that physical exercise just may be the best exercise of all. She cites studies that indicate that physical exercise actually increases blood flow to the brain, which creates increased stem cells growth in the brain and an increase in brain volume in both gray and white matter.

Suggested reading: excerpts from chapter 9, "Keep Moving and Keep Your Wits: Exercise Builds Brains," pp. 129–43.

Opinion: This book was published just in the nick of time for many baby boomers, including one of this book's authors. Suffering with the lost car in the parking lot, the name on the tip of the tongue, the futile trips from one room to another in search of "What?" while all the while finding it increasingly difficult to deal with life's little hassles can cause any aging person to wonder if he or she is really, finally, losing it. It is nice to know that not only are we *not* losing it, there are things that we can actually do to keep ourselves from losing it! An extremely readable, informational, and enjoyable book written about this topic.

Events Prep Series (aka The Sneak Peak)

One of the most difficult parts about events and programs planned for the population at large at a library is that they can seem overwhelming and inaccessible to seniors. While the special *senior services desk* may be there to help with seating issues and more, some libraries do not have the luxury of a separate station for seniors. In any case, it is appropriate to help prepare for library events in a more meaningful way and drum up some excitement. The coordinator should choose appropriate events that are occurring at the library, whether direct library programming or any event occurring on the library grounds. Event prep is a fun hour of taking a closer look at the theme of the event, such as the history of that theme, the guest speakers, a preview, the resources in the library related to that topic, the logistics of the event, or just what to expect. The intent of this program is to get patrons excited, enable inclusion, and allow seniors to have a more in-depth experience with the event.

Partnerships

Most of the legwork for partnerships has been taken care of for this program. Already established partnerships for upcoming events can be contacted to see if they would provide guest speakers, refreshments, or a sneak peak for the seniors.

Example

For an upcoming arts festival taking place on the library grounds, the events prep hour could include discount coupons for senior attendees, a sneak preview of a presenting artist or another speaker, a discussion of the map and parking, and even weather reports. It could also highlight other art events that are upcoming around the city, like a gallery stroll, or an artist open house. It should include a handout of free art museums and even art competitions.

Learning Local Series

The Culture of Your City through Art, History, and Architecture

Part of what is fun about being retired or having more free time is taking the time to enjoy and learn about things you only had time to glance at in passing before. This series takes a closer look at the unique culture of your area. Seniors will have the opportunity to take a closer look at the city or countryside around them, one they may have known all their life or are just getting acquainted with. Through library resources, old photos, guest speakers, and more, they will learn more about your area's unique history, interesting art and art community, and even architecture. This program should be conducted in conjunction with the local historical society and/or history museum.

Partnerships

Partnerships for this series should be the local historical society, local history enthusiasts, architectural history professors, history students, local artists, art societies, and gallery owners.

Possible Topics

- Local cowboys or local poets or even cowboy poets (our favorite!)
- Local architecture—historic or modern
- Local myths and legends
- Local natural sights like hot springs, caves, or archaeological sites
- Local historic events
- Local artists and art shows
- Local celebrities
- Local events—arts, music, and education
- Local music and musicians

Staycations

Unfortunately, travel is often not a possibility for many older adults due to financial or health concerns. Thanks to technology, the world is a smaller place, which means such limitations are now much less limiting. This program can also function to get those who can travel excited and informed. This program will feature one travel destination each month; the places should be based on the availability of guest speakers such as willing library staff, members of the Friends of the Library, and also the requests of patrons. Each event will showcase photographs, first-person accounts, videos both online and in collection, as well as websites, music, and excerpts from the library collection. Food and drink that is culturally relevant can be provided. The event can also feature cultures that span geographic regions. For those who can travel, these programs can serve as a preparation for their travels. They can send in updates and photos to the senior website as a fun connection idea.

Promotion

Local travel agents could earn free advertisement and promotion. Friends of the Library and the librarians can facilitate group speakers who have traveled extensively for fun or professionally.

Story Bee

Based on the magazine *Reminisce* and the *Storycorps* program, older adults can now have a local group to share stories and pictures of their lives based on a variety of themes. Each themed event will include books and materials from the library collection that highlight a theme such as the 1950s or the Great Depression. Seniors can use their own stories or interview friends and family for sharing.

Note: If there is enough enthusiasm, they can take this project to new heights, creating their own magazine or individual zines (online self-published works). This would focus on seniors as producers of information, rather than just consumers, in print or online format. A printable form would mean using a layout program like Adobe In Design or any free online layout program, and an online form such as a blog or free website. Additionally, when *Storycorps* comes to your city, older adults should be informed in advance, invited to participate, and given any support that will help them participate with ease.

See *Reminisce* magazine: http://www.reminisce.com
See Storycorps: http://storycorps.org/

Partnerships

Local bakeries and restaurants should be contacted for donations, as they would get free advertisement and promotion. Solicit long-term local businesses since they were around and might be part of the told stories.

Ideas

- Best adventures ever had: What adventures do you look forward to as well?
- Children ask questions of seniors
- Christmas memories
- Favorite vacations
- First memory
- Funniest memories
- How your parents met
- How you met your spouse
- Inspiring stories or who inspired you
- Most interesting part of history you experienced
- Seniors as grandparents: Found common ground with today's youth? Times change?
- Teens interview seniors for school project

Video Games

Video games have become popular with the retirement crowd. They are fun, group oriented, interactive, physical, and easy to learn. Many seniors enjoy playing games with their grandchildren and each other. If there is not funding for a gaming system for senior programming, a gaming system originally purchased for the teen department can be borrowed since it is probably mostly unused during school hours on weekdays and early morning on the weekends. Tournaments and intergenerational programming are a must! Free play is allowed during nonevent time. Event days will include refreshments and prizes.

We suggest using the following platforms:

Nintendo Wii or the Xbox 360 Kinect

Both of these systems have many multiplayer games that are interactive and motion triggered.

Partnerships

Partnerships for this program can be local game stores for tech support. Prizes could be solicited from local businesses such as game stores but also local businesses who would like to boost sales to senior patrons (i.e., Game Stop).

Suggested Games

Choose games that are interactive and can have multiple players. Try to purchase games used for a huge price break. All games listed are multiplayer.

Kinect Games: http://en.wikipedia.org/wiki/List_of_Kinect_games

Brunswick Bowling
Deca Sports
EA Sports Active 2.0
Game Party: In-Motion (includes mini games like horseshoes and bean bag toss)
Kinect Adventures (includes creative mini-games like River Rush)
Kinect Sports (includes bowling, hurdles, sprint, javelin, discus throw, and long jump)
Virtua Tennis 4

Wii Games: http://en.wikipedia.org/wiki/List_of_Wii_games

Are You Smarter than a Fifth Grader?
Big Beach Sports
Carnival Games
Classic British Motor Racing
Deca Sports 1, 2, or 3 (includes a variety of sports from football, basketball, badminton, curling, and figure skating)
Family Feud Decades
Family Gameshow
Family Games
Hasbro Family Game Night (includes classics: Connect Four, Battleship, Boggle, Sorry, and Yahtzee)
Mario Kart (a fast-paced racing game; it can be hard to follow for beginners but is great fun!)
Medieval Games (includes sword fighting, jousting, archery, and catapulting)
Monopoly
Monopoly Streets
Pinball Hall of Fame
Smarty Pants (quiz game)
Summer Athletics (includes 25 summer sports from sprinting, hurdles, cycling, archery, javelin, hammer throwing, swimming, and diving)
Super Swing Golf
Table Football
Table Tennis
Trivial Pursuit
Virtua Tennis 2009
Wacky World of Sports (includes hilarious and creative games such as Furniture Racing and Extreme Ironing)
We Love Golf
Wii Chess
Wii Music
Wii Party
Wii Play
Wii Sports Resort (includes a variety of sports: archery, cycling, canoeing, power cruising, and wake-boarding)
Wonderworld Amusement Park (rides and games for multiplayer)

TIPS FOR CREATING YOUR OWN PROGRAMMING

Consistency

When program planning, our first recommendation is consistency. If you have a senior programming day each month or even week, always keep the same day, time, and starting place. Nothing is worse than making an effort to attend an event and discovering that you have the wrong room or you've come too late. This is especially important for older adults because times and dates will be easier to remember if they are consistent. It makes it easier to plan for events that your senior patrons will look forward to.

Combine Patron Needs and Wants with Your Expertise

Basing program creation from the needs and wants of your patrons and potential patrons is a sure path to success. Your environmental scans and surveys are an essential part of choosing and creating the right programs to entice your patrons into the library. Now there is that gray area where you, as a trained experienced librarian, have an amazing program idea and wonder if the patrons just don't know if they need it or want it. We say . . . go for it! If it's a well-constructed program and actively promoted through marketing, then it's time to put your training, skills, and knowledge of your patron base to work. Evaluation will be the key to its repeat in the future. As you build a fan base, patrons will come to the programming because they know they will have a great time no matter the program you are putting on.

Think Local

The best way to have a successful series of programs is to have the built-in ability to pull from a broad spectrum of local resources. This way, it is easy to provide guest speakers and recommend continuing education on the subject. For example, it might sound fun to do a program on flamenco dancing, but if there are no flamenco dancers or similar resources in your area, it is going to be a difficult road to find the things you need for your program, including guest speakers. While you might try to create it anyway, the essential component, described earlier in this chapter, of *continuing the journey* can be difficult for patrons without these local connections.

Scour the In-House Resources

More than you believed possible might be right there at your disposal—from books to magazines to journal articles to random employees or volunteers with something to offer. Remember that staff survey we suggested back in chapter 1? Find out the special skills and hobbies of all your employees, even the janitors! They are a great free resource and may be thrilled to be active participants as a change to their routine or may be more comfortable with offering advice only. The seniors section of your library is not an island, so reach out!

Find Those Free Outside Resources

- Start with the small easy stuff . . . free Web resources. Some may be of use during the presentation while the others can be a part of your additional resources list.
- Next, move on to free speakers from local organizations. Speakers may even be persuaded to come if they can leave marketing material for their services. Just be sure to put an assortment of all services available . . . we cannot play favorites.
- Next, think about the materials needed and solicit local businesses for items that may be helpful.
- Found objects are great. Have your staff keep an eye out for free items curbside. One of the authors found 30 complete years worth of *National Geographic* magazines on a curbside in nice boxes all ready for art projects or other fun uses! This tactic has also worked for picture frames and even pots for plants. Get creative!

- Grants are an ongoing option. Don't wait to find one that matches your program; create programming around grants, as well.
- As a final thought, see if you can procure items from a local thrift store or dollar store.

Whatever you are able to do for your seniors will make their lives more interesting. You should also share your successful programs with other librarians, giving them the same kinds of information we have provided for you.

CHAPTER 5

Promote and Gain a Fan Base

Confidently marketing all your library programs and services effectively is essential. Successful marketing creates connections with current patrons and functions as outreach for garnering new patrons. Your connections can excite voters and keep your library on the radar with those who have funding power. The best advice we can give is, "Hit them with all you've got, and then some." Today, there are multiple avenues readily available to reach out to your audience; best of all, there are even more ways for them to reach right back to you! The following chapter will explore a range of marketing tools, from traditional methods, such as fliers, to more technological means such as Twitter. We have endeavored to provide you with a comprehensive list of options that includes all our very best ideas and suggestions. You know your community best, and we hope that this list allows you to broaden your promotional horizons and improve the success of your program. Additionally, we think it's important to create a fan base, a group of patrons who are passionate about making your library and its programs successful. This is the part where they come to you!

Initiating a patron-library relationship can be as simple as "requesting friends" on the program's Facebook page or getting to know all the regulars by name. What it can lead to is much greater, such as wonderful volunteers and active voters. This fan base is the foundation of your program and is fundamental for keeping your program alive, especially in the face of adversity. Creating and fostering these relationships can mean the difference between a mediocre senior program and a profoundly successful community impact.

A note about stepping on toes: depending on the size of your facility, there may already be someone assigned to marketing the library. If you are in a branch, the system may indeed have a marketing guru. Our best advice is to come up with your dream plan and work with the marketing department to accomplish the bigger tasks while you endeavor to make some of the more detailed and creative programs successful. The benefits of working together are many. While the marketing budget may cover some of your ideas for senior programs, it might not cover all of them. Working with the marketing team means someone else will do some of the work, which is a good thing, and the marketing guru may already have established relationships with media outlets. Best of all, sharing the workload may gain you an important fan.

THE MARKETING MIND-SET

Understanding the mind-set of your target group is an important first step in customizing your marketing plan. In creating a marketing plan for a senior program, you will need to learn more about the two age groups—baby boomers and senior citizens. Understanding the similarities and differences will allow you to better determine which routes will be most effective for marketing in your area.

Marketing to Baby Boomers

In a *USA Today* article, "Big-Spending Baby Boomers Bend the Rules of Marketing," Matt Thornhill, 50, founder of the Boomer Project, a specialty research firm, suggests that the average marketing firm has forgotten that people over 50—including people *well* over 50, too—still have dreams. This kind of forgetting about the dreams of older folks can also be found in libraries. We tend to focus on youth services and the promotion of reading and programming for children, and we forget that older adults still have informational and educational needs. They still have dreams, which the library and all it has to offer can help make come true. The article goes on to say that marketers have to be careful not to make older people feel old and suggests the following ways to improve how you reach out to older adults, particularly baby boomers:

- Make them feel *good*. Feeling good is something that comes naturally to us when we are young—feeling good physically, feeling good emotionally, feeling as if we have all the time in the world to make our dreams come true. As we age and the reality that all our dreams may not come true sets in, the good feelings of our youth are still there, they just need to be coaxed out a little bit. We have to be reminded that it's never too late to pursue our dreams. Marketing for baby boomers, in particular, should appeal to their sense of fun and adventure. Remember, these are the movers and shakers of another era. This is also the generation that started a cultural revolution, so appealing to their sense of social justice or connecting them with a cause works as well.
- Make them feel hip. Feeling hip becomes increasingly difficult as we get older. When you're younger, it's easy to define your hipness by wearing the latest fashion trend, no matter how ghastly, which is frequently inappropriate for older folk. Besides, many older people wouldn't be caught dead in many current fashions for a number of reasons. Use images of older people wearing shoes other than those that are horribly sensible or dressed in something other than suspenders and baseball caps in your print marketing. Using images of older people wearing hip, modern eyewear is a plus. Little things make a difference.
- Make them feel smart. In general, older people are smart. Yes, we hear the rare story of older people committing crimes and doing crazy things, but most of the mischief in the world is committed by those 60 and under. Age brings wisdom, and, for some people, it makes them tired, so there's little likelihood of them engaging in a prank such as toilet papering a neighbor's lawn for fun. Even the hardest of individuals tend to soften in old age. We all know of the tough drill-sergeant dad who became an old softie with his grandchildren. This can be attributed to the wisdom of age, and you should appeal to that side of aging when it is appropriate. You don't want to advertise every single program or service as being geared toward Yoda himself, but you do want to emphasize the wisdom and smarts of older people.
- Make them feel techie. Tied in to the idea of being smart, in this day and age this means being considered tech savvy. The more you can help your older adults learn about new technologies and use those technologies to market to them, the better they will feel about themselves and technology. Teach them about Twitter and then market programs through Twitter as well as standard marketing venues (Horovitz, 2010).

We like these suggestions because all the feelings described in the article come more readily to young people. It is important for older people, especially baby boomers, to still feel hip, smart, technologically savvy, and just plain good, and libraries can do their part to make that happen.

Marketing to All Older Adults

In an article called "Marketing Knows No Age Limit," Jessica Tsai offers notes from a keynote address given by Ken Dychtwald, a former psychologist and gerontologist and now president and chief executive officer of Age Wave, a consultancy specializing in helping companies target baby boomers and mature adults. In this address, Dychtwald suggests that in marketing to older adults, there are certain keys to follow:

- Be aspirational, not desperational. Focus on the dreams and aspirations of older people. Being older doesn't necessarily mean being desperate. Baby boomers, in particular, have accrued more wealth and will have more wealth in their senior years than any other generation. They are still dreaming and planning for tomorrow.
- Have fun and laugh with, not at, older people. Poking fun at any generation is just not cool, and with older people who might be feeling marginalized and left behind about so many things, technology in particular, it is doubly unacceptable.
- Understand generational anchoring. Generational anchoring might be thought of as sentimentality, but guess what? It isn't. It is simply appealing to the things that were important to people in their developing, coming-of-age years. Just like many older adults like the music of the 1930s and 1940s and now younger seniors like the rock and roll of the 1960s and 1970s, one day older people will be bopping their heads to rap music. Lady Gaga will be played on the oldies station. It's just what happens as time keeps on ticking. Don't snub the idea of appealing to what was important and fun to folks when they were coming of age; instead, use it to promote appropriate services and programs.
- Target mind-set, lifestyle, and life stage, not age. Focus on the stage that the person is currently in instead of chronological age. Create and promote programs to new retirees, the elderly, and baby boomers and use appropriate images and language for each group. Use lifestyle and stage as a means of marketing and for creating your programs and services as well (Tsai, 2009).

MARKETING TOOLS (aka GETTING THEIR ATTENTION)

We all know you have your old marketing standbys, which are probably cheap and easy. They probably work just fine. So why are you reading this chapter? We hope you want to do more than reaffirm old methods, but instead would like to find out about what's new and fresh. In either case, we think it's time for librarians to spice things up a bit. Today's world is chock full of marketing, everyone is constantly barraged by media and promotions, and the only way for your library to stand out, well, is to stand out! Add some new promotional routes, get motivated, be active and ingenious, and create a marketing plan that is as exciting and dynamic as the programs and services you have created. Not listed in any particular order, these methods range from tried and true to downright fresh off the press.

When choosing your intended routes of promotion, it is important to keep your broader audience in mind. We all know that senior patrons, both users and nonusers, are your intended audience. Those are the people you want to see at your programs and filling up your seniors area, and here we go again with the dreaming big. Reaching a very select population requires more than just a drop of water; it requires a hose. This means you shouldn't just market to those over the age of 65, even though they are your main intended audience, because every person who sees, hears, or reads your marketing material is connected in some way to a senior citizen. Community gatekeepers, news outlet personnel, friends, family, caregivers, children, and grandchildren all know seniors. They will do your marketing for you! So while a senior may not follow you on Twitter, a marketing director at the local health department might, and he or she has a very broad reach, perhaps broader than yours, and is more than willing to pass on information. A local nurse may follow your event blog and relate it to all of her clients and their families. The bottom line is that while seniors may not be well connected to the media of today, they are well connected in their communities, so more is better when mass-marketing.

Word of Mouth (WOM)

In *Bite-Sized Marketing*, Nancy Dowd and colleagues suggest that word-of-mouth (WOM) marketing can be the driving force behind your library's successful marketing strategy. It is a well-known fact that we trust the recommendations of others regarding the best sites to see, things to do, and restaurants at which to eat, even down to the dishes that we should order at specific restaurants. We share recommended reading all the time with those of similar reading tastes and share where we shop for specific items, so we know that, yes, WOM does work. In order to have good WOM about your library, you need to have good things to offer and good customer service to back up your offerings. Since you have hopefully been working on ideas for creating a great senior program, a little WOM might be just thing at this point.

These are three of the basic elements Dowd and colleagues suggest you use to start your WOM campaign:

- Identify those with influence in the community who have a positive relationship with the library.
- Offer simple-to-communicate messages about the library for the influencers to spread.
- Host a conversation about your customers' needs and opinions and be sure to include some of those positive influencers in the group.

Telling the story—the complete story—of the services your library offers and empowering library users to do the same may just be one of the most effective means of marketing that *no money* can buy.

Local News Outlets

These are an important part of your marketing scheme but can be tough to break into. While news consumers should see community interest stories, such as your upcoming author event, it's the crime and disaster stories that are popular and catch their attention. It is important to keep trying as the effort alone will help you find and establish relationships with local reporters. They may grow to love you as you tirelessly submit story after story, and the next thing you know, your library and your program will have finally made the television news!

Remember that in most instances, news reporters are not going to be knocking at your door for news of the library, and if they are, it could be for all the wrong reasons. It's up to you to foster a good working relationship with local news agencies, which means keeping them informed about library events and developing a good relationship with them. Sometimes they might ask questions that are more difficult to answer, but if you want them to help you create good buzz, you might have to occasionally "face the music" on some sticky issue—but that's the focus of another book. It's far better to be friendly and available to local news outlets than cold and unapproachable.

Some ideas for newspaper submission: blurbs of upcoming events and programs, new and exciting services, and especially reports of success. Media outlets are all interconnected, so oftentimes the articles you submit, if published, will be posted online as well to the newspaper's own website. From there, they can be picked up for publication and referenced nationally or even worldwide.

Fee vs. Free

While inclusion in many local news outlets can and should be free, there are some cost options that are worth pursuing, including radio spots and columns in local papers. Check with your library marketing at large to find out if your senior program can be included in any such options they are currently invested in. Otherwise, do some price checking and decide if the rates are compatible with your department's budget.

Newspapers: Print Format

While the trend is toward online news among younger people, you can be assured that at this point in time, many older adults still subscribe to the local newspaper in its print format. We know this time may be short-lived, but right now, you can still reach seniors with newspaper ads and articles.

In many communities, the news of the library is a weekly or monthly column. If this is not the case in your community, you should find out how you can make that happen by contacting your local newspaper. A book review column is a standard in many local newspapers and is frequently written by the local librarian. In smaller communities, where big news doesn't happen every day, you will obviously have less competition for space in the newspaper. When writing for your local paper, be sure to include those programs and services that appeal to older adults, such as events offered by a different department at your library. Don't forget to go one step smaller in newsprint publications and include neighborhood newsletters, free city weekly papers, senior journals, and community calendars. Send out any and all worthy articles and blurbs to your contacts at these outlets as well.

News: Television Format

How do you get the attention of the television news for an event? Find a contact and keep him or her informed on a monthly or even weekly basis. Be sure to include all the selling points about what's coming up or has already happened successfully, such as the largest program ever, large expected attendance, a famous guest speaker, or something new or exciting. Have a flier or two handy with your contact information and that of the program and any blogs, websites, and phone numbers, as your contact may choose to include this at the end of the program or simply want to keep in touch.

Radio

Local stations have done their listener research. Their sales department would be only too glad to spout off a giant list of statistics to you. It's great information and can help you choose a station with which to advertise. Best of all, you could find a locally funded radio station that would give you a free 15- to 30-second radio spot once or twice a month. In exchange, this station could be played at a low volume in the senior area, and fliers for their upcoming events could be posted in a handouts area.

Printed Marketing Material

Printed materials are a traditional form of marketing for libraries. They enable a patron to take away information as a reminder or to present to others who might be interested. They are useful to give in stacks to community gatekeepers and leave at popular haunts for seniors. Other printed material is suitable for displays, like posters and banners, while still other creations can be given out as reference items.

Library Newsletter(s)

Always include your department information and updates in the library-wide newsletter. Find out how much space is allotted for your department, and make the most of it. Always turn in your submissions early, and make friends with the person in charge of its construction.

An option for larger or new departments in larger libraries is to create your own smaller newsletter. This is a must if your library does not have its own newsletter or if that newsletter is only printed rarely. However, with smaller libraries, a newsletter may be a more difficult challenge. What is nice about creating your own newsletter in any situation is that the electronically created text can function as copyover material for the department website or email notifications.

In any case, include as much information as possible or allowed. Always start with the events schedule for the next month, including any special features or eye catchers, perhaps a speaker's photograph, and always include teasers about what's in the works or coming up. Other inclusion suggestions are a featured book review, a featured website review, highlighting a patron, highlighting a service, focusing on a librarian, and exploring the success of a past program or when your program was in the local news.

Fliers and Handouts

These handheld pieces of paper are a breeze to pick up, are easy to read, and readily attach to any refrigerator or dashboard. They should provide clear and concise information as well as contact information. They should be specific to the senior department.

Essential Fliers

1. Monthly events schedule flier: If you go further out than monthly, you risk scheduling conflicts and unforeseen events that can lead to time and date changes. Any special services available for an individual program should be noted along with contact information to arrange the service. Also be sure to include contact information for the event coordinator. You may want to do one of two things: list library-wide programs that may be of interest, but not ones in conflicting time slots, and/or provide a website link to the library-wide events schedule.
2. General senior flier: This functions as an advertisement for your department by itself. Make sure to incorporate your department's theme with eye-catching words and visuals. Include all forms of contact information.
3. Services flier: Patrons would like to know what makes your programming special and how they will benefit from the programs, especially if they have special needs or a disability. Fliers for services you offer may be carried off by one patron to a nonpatron as a form of proof ("See, they will walk you to your car, if you need it!").

Nonessential, but Handy, Fliers

1. Event flier: If you have a big event coming up, by all means, provide a single flier just for that event. Include what makes it special, a photo of the guest or topic, and all pertinent contact information. These fliers are handy because they can be provided to a very select group for a marketing bump. For example, a flier for a health program can be delivered or provided to public health offices, local Medicaid/Medicare provider offices, and clinics.
2. Informational handouts: If you ran a program with a popular topic and the handouts went like hotcakes, it's time to pile up some on your reference desk. These can be tech topics such as how to use email or random information lists such as a list of garden stores that sell native plants. Ideally, these lists are also provided on your senior website and would include active links to other websites and even videos.
3. Community services and referral information handouts: These should ideally have their own kiosk, but if you live in a small community, they can certainly be featured in the mix on the reference desk. These are best obtained for free from local government offices and maybe from some nonprofits, but when not available, make your own.

Posters

Posters can be really similar to your fliers in content and scope, but with one big difference—artwork. As they are bigger and meant to be longer lasting, invest in some great artwork. Hold a competition among library staff and volunteers or ask for patron contributions. Always include credit and contact information so they can benefit as well, or use clipart from either free sites or sites with a nominal fee. Best yet, create your own posters using staff photography and a great photo-editing or layout program. With washes, filters, and font styles, you can get pretty creative without being a full artist yourself. Keep in mind the design basics and your intended placement. All posters should feature eye-catching colors and images, easily readable large text, and all the pertinent information. If the posters are to be placed in the library, text can be intentionally vague, referring patrons to the department for more information, where the librarian can act as a salesperson for the program and offer some of those concierge services. If they are for the community at large, include a bit more information. Price out printing costs in your community and from online websites. You might be surprised that printing a poster as a large-sized photograph can be cheaper than getting a poster printed as a "poster" at the print shop! The quality will be higher, and it can often be ordered online.

Bookmarks

These tiny little scraps are cheap to print, easy to hand out, helpful for patrons, and can contain a wealth of rotating information on a wide variety of topics. Print up new ones on heavy cardstock each week or as needed. Bookmarks can also be printed on the backs of book pages that are going to be thrown away, especially illustrated pages. Access to a laminator machine is a plus, but not necessary. Give these bookmarks out like candy by offering them at the reference desk and in stacks around the department as well as hiding them in books on the shelves.

TECHNOLOGY

Whether a senior patron is Web fluent yet or not, it is imperative that marketing through technology become a vital part of your marketing scheme. Why? Community gatekeepers, friends, family, caregivers, children, and grandchildren are all connected to technology. They will do your marketing for you! This is a form of viral marketing, which involves using social networks to market in an attempt to have your message self-replicate and spread without further involvement on your part. The most popular route for this usually involves emails, text messages, and social media of all kinds. So it is incredibly important to keep current and active with promotion through technology as it can lead to some of the best exposure for your program. Just like WOM, information can spread through technology like wildfire.

Those seniors who are current on technology or simply excited learners will love the technology components of your marketing. It will keep them completely up-to-date on programming and events. They can easily forward or pass on email and links to people they know. Best of all, it gives them a way to connect with your department if they are ill or even out of the country!

Websites

Make use of any online space you are given. Provide updates, and create a wonderful working relationship with your IT department or Web programmer to ensure that your programs and notices are included on the library's general website.

Having a senior department-specific website is the ideal. Your website can offer so much more than the single page on the library's website could afford, as discussed in previous chapters. The website will function as an invaluable marketing tool as well. Again, the key to this site is that you and your staff must be capable of updating it. If you have to wait for an IT tech to do it, and it is not working out, get permission to branch out on your own with a low-cost Web host. Even better, get a grant for a custom website! Many Web-development companies create custom websites that are client updatable and changeable.

Your website should include an events tab, a calendar, a programming tab, a services tab, and plenty of contact information. Also, putting up reviews, photos, and videos of prior successful events is a great way to market for repeat or similar events. Unsure potential patrons can get a feel for what to expect from the programming and will hopefully become interested enough to bring a friend and come by.

Email List

Just like the website, this is a must. Have a clipboard on the reference desk as well as a sign-up box on the website. Email lists are for keeping patrons up-to-date on everything current. Your email list can also feature spotlights on upcoming speakers and long-term library staff. The key here is not to send too many emails. Twice a month should be perfect, unless there is a cancellation or added event. Make sure patrons can easily unsubscribe.

Facebook Page

We already know that learning how to create their own Facebook account (http://www.facebook.com) is a huge hit with senior patrons. This is the best way to give them practice in becoming a Facebook fan or friend, and you show them by having a senior Facebook site at the library. The heart of connecting with your patrons is interaction, so initiate conversations via questions, requests for ideas and feedback, as well as polls. This allows patrons to engage in a two-way conversation with you and allows them to have a role in the success of your department. You provide news and updates, and they can give instant feedback. Since you have already created this same information for the website, clicking over to Facebook and updating is a quick task. You can also post videos and photographs here.

If you can start by quickly obtaining over 25 fans, this will allow you to set up a special username that comes along with a shortened URL. We found this to be easiest if you have library staff become fans, too. Your senior page should be updated as frequently as possible. If not daily status updates, then before and after every single event. Your fans can review upcoming events and then choose to share them instantly with their friends with one swift button click. Most people have many Facebook friends, so your updates and postings can reach even more people. As a bonus, as the Facebook page creator, you will have access to a variety of statistics via Facebook Insights, including viewer data.

Twitter Account

This is where the fun begins. A bit less formal and more free-flowing than a blog or a Facebook account, a Twitter account (http://www.twitter.com) lets you "tweet" random short tidbits and thoughts in 140 characters or fewer. It can be linked directly to your senior Facebook page. The reference desk librarians should be logged into the Twitter account while they are on the clock. The list is endless as to what they can tweet. They can make comments on anticipated books that are on order, provide links to news stories of interest, or express ideas still in their heads for upcoming programming, which is a great way to network and gauge for interest at the same time. They can type out verbal compliments they just received about the senior program or even just express their excitement for a program they are helping with that night or in the immediate future. A Twitter account gives the department or your senior program, when it isn't a separate department, a life of its own, with a breathing, thinking mind behind it. The interaction with patrons and potential patrons is very casual and invites easy feedback and essential interaction. Try it out for six months or so, and see if your following grows. Be sure to promote it from your webpage, from your senior department Facebook page, through handouts, as well as verbally.

THE "CONTAGIOUS CURIOSITY" MARKETING STRATEGY

Here is a wild variation of a viral/guerilla marketing campaign that we have dubbed *Contagious Curiosity.* Contagious Curiosity (CC) is the perfect way to challenge the norm and really take your program to a new level. Plus, CC is just downright creative and innovative. The goal of CC is to create underground buzz through your marketing material that spreads through word of mouth, encouraging new patrons to come in and creating excitement and knowledge about your department and its programming.

The premise is that natural human curiosity is a powerful tool and that it should be used more often in marketing. This strategy is accomplished by creating marketing materials that employ *intriguing but vague* concepts that elicit *confusion leading to curiosity*. For example, there are tons of cars in my hometown that have a *Ragnar* sticker, with no other information, on their expensive eco-friendly and even upper-class sports utility vehicles. I was constantly curious about this word and the unique logo design and even went so far as to associate it with something rich and special. I finally found out it was for a relay running competition, and although I won't be participating, if someone were to ask for marathon suggestions, this one is burned into my brain. Marketing like this also provides a sense of exclusivity, which also breeds curiosity—when people keep seeing a logo everywhere, it feels as if everyone knows about it but them, and they naturally think it is special and want to find out more.

So it's time to use the unique theme for your senior department to create a marketing concept that is dramatic, fun, intriguing, and that stands out from the crowd. The key is *not* to provide all the details; the potential patron must bridge the gap, creating an instant bond between themselves and your product. Once they find out about your senior department, it will not only be memorable but also have a number of positive associations built into their thoughts about it—as something exclusive and unique.

The John Cotton Dana Awards are given out yearly by the American Library Association to libraries that have created innovative public relations campaigns. The 2011 award winners had amazing ideas that were quite viral. The Worthington Libraries in Ohio rebranded themselves via the theme *Find Yourself Here*, which included a series of posters and T-shirts that played off that central theme, such as *Find Bacon Here*. The posters were bold and demanded attention; they were also quirky and fun.

An example product would be a series of attention-catching, bright, *humorous* bumper stickers that would include a tiny notation for the senior department website listed at the bottom. Again, any marketing along these lines should play off your unique name or theme. Note: wearable items for sale at the library such as bags and shirts work just as well as free posters and buttons. Often people who are not senior patrons, or even patrons at all, will want access to them! Here are some fun and silly examples to get those creative juices flowing:

"Solar Seniors—So bright they can read in the dark"
"Solar Seniors—Growing reading without fossil fuels"
"Solar Seniors—Books so hot they sizzle"
"Solar Seniors—Heating up your day, naturally"
"Solar Seniors—Vibrant, Vital, and Voracious readers"

The whole community will be curious and come for a visit, so you'd better have extra items for fun giveaways!

OTHER TIPS AND TRICKS

Create Your Own Buzz

Some tips for making your own news, adapted from *Marketing: A How-to-Do-It Manual for Librarians* by Suzanne Walters, include the following:

- Tie in your programs and services with current events. If a new statistic on aging is released in the news, use that statistic to write an article about your services for seniors.
- Use events, perhaps National Library Week, to promote your library and its services for patrons of all ages, including seniors.
- Do some programs related to holidays. Since there will be plenty of news articles about Veterans Day, Memorial Day, Mothers Day, Fathers Day, and so on, you might as well add one more story to the group: the story of what you are doing for the older adults in your library on the holiday theme.

Let contacts/community gatekeepers from local senior groups, senior centers, retirement communities, and retirement low-income housing choose which of your marketing materials they would like to have at their individual facility. They could choose from fliers, handouts, posters, Web links, email lists, and word-processing documents for inclusion in their own marketing. Sponsors and partners groups should be encouraged to allow departmental marketing materials to be displayed at their facility/business, just as you display their sponsorship at your events.

Fine-tuning your marketing plan based on customization via evaluation will allow you to keep fresh and current. Use those methods which have proven their worth as a foundation basis for your efforts. Evaluate at the end of each calendar year or budget year.

CONCLUSION

The relationship between marketing and creating a fan base is subtle and overlaps in many places. In the past, traditional marketing only provided information, enticement, and incentives. The marketing of today encourages interaction, creating bridges. By using those methods that allow for interaction, such as Facebook and Twitter, your department is creating lasting relationships with your patrons, which in turn spread out into the community. Feedback and participation are nearly instantaneous. While knowing the names of all of your regular patrons is wonderful, by using technology, you can build a whole new world of fans from community gatekeepers to senators, teens who love your logo, and adults who want to keep tabs on events for their parents. Today's world offers wonderful opportunities to allow our marketing to cross barriers we didn't know existed before. So use your marketing plan to build amazing bridges and promote dynamic interaction.

CHAPTER 6

Everything about Evaluating

This is the time of budget cuts, librarian layoffs, reduced pay, and even library closures. As librarians, we must prove our worth and the value of the departments and programs we run, not only to our own staff, library boards, and governments, but also, far from least, to the public. Evaluation has a pivotal and essential role in creating a record of our journey and a body of proof for our success. When you find out budget cuts are coming or your library director calls you into his or her office and says, "The just cut our budget, why should we keep the senior department?" you will be prepared with more than just words. Use evaluation to find out if your programs and services were successful and effective, as well as their level of impact, and provide evidence for your current success and plans for the future. Set the stage for this process through goal creation.

CREATING GUTSY GOALS

When designing your plans to serve seniors and creating your programs and services, evaluation should be considered and planned for from the start—plan for success by creating dynamic goals for your department as well as your services and programming. Goals should be broad enough to define the overall picture of your intent. Don't forget your own personal professional goals as well! It's important for your public to know your professional accomplishments. In this section, we have defined two types of goals that will be discussed in this chapter: one is department wide and the other is program specific.

A Department-Wide Goal Example

"Enhance learning of local history," a yearlong series of programs and events.

A Program-Specific Goal Example

"Discover the basics of astrology," an hour-long event.

Assessing the Goals Themselves

It is important to consider your goals as one of the items that you must assess on a regular basis. Are your goals clear and concise yet broad enough to allow for major accomplishment? Are they updatable so that year by year they can be renewed as a way of raising the bar? Do they take into account current technology and trends? Are they flexible enough to meet changing library-wide values, goals, and objectives? Are the goals obtainable?

CREATING ACTION-BASED OBJECTIVES

Once you have created your goals, it's time to focus them via the creation of action-based objectives. Just as the name indicates, these objectives are to be action packed. Use words like *create*, *enhance*, and *update* in proliferation. Not only should these action-based objectives allow for multiple paths for staff to meet the goal, but they should be short and sweet and include a timeline. They should be unique among the grouping of objectives, so weed out any redundancies. They should also be readily accomplishable. Objectives can be easily measured through a variety of evaluative methods. Many times it's just a matter of whether that objective was met or not.

A Department-Wide Goal and Objectives Example

Goal: "Enhance learning of local history," a yearlong series of programs and events.
Objectives:

1. By November 1: Accomplish extensive research on potential program topics: Discover local historians or history buffs willing to present; line up at least one per month for 12 months worth of programming.
2. By December 1: Finalize drafts of each monthly program, complete the years' line-up for marketing, finish in-depth preparations and marketing for the first two programs.
3. By January1: Evaluate and update the current collection of local history books—including art and architecture.
4. Monthly: Complete the final preparation of the next month's program.
5. By next summer: Create a display and contest for vintage photos of the city.
6. By fall: Create a map and walking tour of important historic architecture.
7. After the last program: Create a display showing off the success of this yearlong series: include photos, completed projects, and feedback.
8. Pull together and analyze all evaluative information. Address negatives, make improvements, and set new goals. Prepare to present this information in a formal setting.

A Program-Specific Goal and Objectives Example

Goal: "Discover the basics of astrology," an hour-long event.
Objectives:

1. By two months prior to program date: Find and finalize the topics and guest speakers. (Unless this event was part of a yearlong series, and the preparation work was done much in advance for marketing purposes.)
2. By one month prior to event: Have updates to the astrology book collection finished and on display in the senior department for pre-program promotion.

3. By three weeks prior to program: Review and finalize the program. Create and review a list on Web resources related to the topic and the guest speakers. Prepare this final list on a handout as well as for inclusion on the senior departments website.
4. By one week prior to event: Finalize plans for seating, audio, and any other special features. Print all handouts and anticipate and compensate for any potential problems, such as weather.

CREATING OUTCOMES

Through evaluating our objectives, we learned what the staff had accomplished. Now, we must find out how and if the senior department and its programming actually affects the lives of the patrons and the success of the library. The bottom line is that you need to find out if your program had an impact. The only way to discover this is to create a list of achievable outcomes for each goal that are easily measurable. Here are some example measurable outcomes.

A Department-Wide Goal with Outcomes Example

Goal: "Enhance learning of local history," a yearlong series of programs and events.
Outcomes:

1. Patron attendance for the series was higher than 150 people per event.
2. Each program and event in the series, from the first occurrence to the last, increases in attendance.
3. Local history books circulations are up.
4. Hits are up on the "Local History" page of the senior department website.
5. A majority of patrons report, via survey, a positive reaction to the programming.
6. Guest speakers report, via survey, a positive experience and would come speak again if asked.
7. At least 2 of the 12 programs/events garnered media attention.
8. At least 2 of the 12 programs/events were requested to be repeated or expanded on (such as an advanced version of the same topic or creation of an all-ages event on the same topic).

A Program-Specific Goal with Outcomes Example

Goal: "Find out more about astrology," an hour-long event.
Outcomes:

1. Books on astrology and related topics have increased circulation numbers in the month after the program.
2. Hits are made to the "Astrology" program page of the senior department website.
3. A majority of patrons report, via survey, a positive reaction to the programming.
4. Guest speakers report, via survey, a positive experience and would come speak again if asked.
5. Patron attendance was over 50.

COLLECTING EVALUATION EVIDENCE

It is not always immediately clear as to whether a goal or set of goals was met. The goal may have been met in the librarian's mind, but the patrons may have walked away confused or unsatisfied. The only way to find out if the set goals were met or exceeded is to obtain information from a variety of sources. Quantitative information will speak for itself, if it's presented well, but qualitative information adds complexity and is necessary to round out the picture.

Quantitative evidence includes patron attendance logs, requests for repeats of a program, circulation statistics, published news articles, patron survey/feedback forms with ratings and yes/no questions, and hit counts on the senior department website.

Qualitative evidence consists of patron survey/feedback forms with opinion sections, even if you have to bribe with a contest entry; comments on the website; feedback from community gatekeepers and partners; feedback from library staff; your own opinion; and guest speaker feedback with an indication of willingness to speak again.

What it all boils down to is gathering evaluative information from various sources in multiple ways. Combine evaluation methods to get both a broader spectrum of results but also to cover your potential blind spots.

CREATING EVALUATION SURVEYS

You might be wondering why we haven't created sample evaluation surveys for you, and included them in our handy appendix, like we did for the assessment chapter. That is because evaluations need to be customized, and the questions need to correspond directly to your program and service specific goals, objectives, and outcomes. But lucky you, creating great evaluation surveys is incredibly easy! This is because your evaluative questions are a direct product of your proposed outcomes. The questions you ask yourself, your staff, and the attending patrons via your surveys or even personal interviews are pretty much just reworded versions of those outcomes. So you see, you don't have to create anything new—its just basic rewording of one question based on each outcome. You may choose to add some additional questions. These should be qualitative, and can be slightly off topic or simply generic, such as demographic information. Here are a couple of sample evaluation surveys.

A Program-Specific Example of an Evaluation Survey

Goal: "Find out more about astrology," an hour-long event.
Outcomes:

1. Books on astrology and related topics have increased circulation numbers in the month after the program.
2. Hits are made to the "Astrology" program page of the senior department website.
3. A majority of patrons report, via survey, a positive reaction to the programming.
4. Guest speakers report, via survey, a positive experience and would come speak again if asked.
5. Patron attendance was over 50.

Evaluative Questions for Patrons (based directly on the above listed outcomes)

1. After attending this program, do you intend to peruse and/or check out related materials? (Based on outcome 1)
   Yes __
   No __
   Not Sure __
   If yes, what have you learned?
2. After attending this program, do you intend to peruse the topical page on astrology created for this program on our website? (Based on outcome 2)
   Yes __
   No __
   Not Sure __
3. After attending this program, do you believe you learned something about this topic? (Based on outcome 3)
   Yes __
   No __
   Not Sure __

If yes, what did you learn?

4. What was your favorite part of the program? (Based on outcome 3)
5. After attending this program, do you intend to continue your education on this topic via contact with any of the guest speakers? (Based on outcome 4)

    Yes __

    No __

    Not Sure __

    If yes, which one(s):

6. After attending this program, would you come to another program on this same topic area? (For example, a program on Tarot) (Based on loosely on outcome 5)

    Yes __

    No __

    Not Sure __

7. Do you have any other feedback or suggestions for us? (Based on loosely on outcome 3)

Creating an evaluation for your staff is done along similar lines. The questions are quite similar to your outcomes but turned into questions that are asked from a different perspective.

Evaluative Questions for Staff Evaluation

1. Was patron attendance for this program higher or lower than you expected?
2. Are circulations up for astrology and related topics?
3. Are hits up on the "Astrology" page of the senior department website?
4. Did any patrons report via verbal survey an enjoyment of the programming?
5. Did you enjoy the program? Why or why not?
6. Do you believe the patrons enjoyed the program? Why or why not?
7. Do you believe the program should be conducted again in the future?
8. What do you believe could be done to improve the program?
9. Any other thoughts?

FOSTERING AN OPEN DIALOGUE

On all survey or feedback forms, be sure to ask if you have permission to post quotes online, either including a name or to be printed anonymously. Then be sure to keep a running log of positive feedback on the website with dates! Don't hesitate to add negative feedback with a note from you about how that problem was taken into consideration promptly and what is being done about it. Be sure to survey community gatekeepers and partners; they have professional opinions that are invaluable. Even patron attendance counts tallied by the senior center can point to how well your gatekeeper relationship is faring with the activities director there.

Speaker feedback is essential. They will not come back if they were confused about the details of their presentation—such as where, when, and what—if they felt unwelcome, or if there was poor attendance. Make sure your communication skills are at their best if you want to maintain a roster of great guest speakers. Send out a speaker feedback survey every time, along with a wonderful thank you letter!

ASSESSING THE EVIDENCE

1. Start by examining your outcomes one by one.
2. What evidence do you have that this goal was met? Log and record.

3. If a goal was unmet, what can be done differently to meet it? Create a plan.
4. Do any goals need to be revised or scrapped?
5. Does the evaluation information reveal any new potential goals?
6. Is there any other pertinent information that could be used to improve a program or your department?

Be sure to log and record any changes you make. How will you know if you have made an improvement in this particular area? Why, by creating a goal, of course! For example, if a patron commented on the inability to see the projector screen, it should lead to a goal with action items to obtain a higher quality screen that functions better in the library's lighting.

UPDATING PROGRAMS AND SERVICES BASED ON EVALUATION

Once all your information is gathered, it's time to put it all together. Make sure your results are in a presentation-style form that is easily understandable by nonlibrary persons of interest, such as stakeholders and future funders. It's important to keep your goals, objectives, and outcomes fluid and updated. Here are some tips.

Keep them current: Community needs and wants change, so don't get stuck recycling the same old programs year after year. Keep digital copies of every program, and keep them updated. Changes can be prompted by news, new community surveys, feedback, and great ideas.

Broaden the perspective: If your program ended up being one sided in a multisided issue, consider branching out next time you present it or conducting a program on the alternative viewpoint.

Use patron feedback to set a course: If patrons kept asking your nutrition expert nonstop questions about weight loss, it's a sure sign of interest in that topic. Always learn something from each evaluation.

Follow-up: Often patrons will have a surge of interest in a program topic, so if you hit a wildly popular note, create a follow-up program to take advantage of the topic's popularity. A variation on the theme or an expansion will have a built-in group of attendees and, maybe, their friends!

Low attendance: Low attendance for a program or low use of a service can be related to marketing. Make sure to assess your marketing before you scrap a program entirely. It can also be tied to bad timing, such as weather, a concurrent community event, or even a TV show finale! So do a thorough evaluation before throwing a low-attendance program into the dust bin.

DEALING WITH BAD FEEDBACK OR CONTROVERSY

Did the program get complaints? Are they justified? How can you better round out the viewpoints expressed in your program? How can you offer a solution? Is the program worth keeping despite the complaints? What evidence do you have that it should have been a popular topic or should have gone better? Before you discard it, think about this: sometimes success isn't measured by the outcome, but rather the work it took to get there. It's not so impressive to get a helicopter ride to stand on a mountain peak, but it's a higher measure of success to have reached the summit by hiking all the way up with determination and skill. This means that the process of evaluating, revising, and reattempting to achieve a successful program is just as important as having a successful program. The benefits of this can stretch into all aspects of your job. So rework and update and try again. It might end up being your most popular program! Some examples to think about include the following.

Boring: The topic was important, but you and your patrons went to sleep. Consider combining the topic with a more entertaining companion. For example, a lecture on diabetes could be combined with a sugar-free cooking demonstration.

Too popular: Okay, this is our greatest wish! The first thing to consider is whether the topic will still be popular in the next year or so. If you believe it's just starting to pick up steam, then get planning for next year's repeat. Add materials, keep an ear open for guest speakers, and keep tabs on the most enthusiastic patrons. They might even be presenters by the next program!

Consider space issues and other technicalities. How can they be remedied to provide for a larger or noisy crowd next year? This is the prime time to start planning so that you don't forget all the little details.

BRINGING IT ALL TOGETHER

We are back to the beginning. You are having your fateful meeting in the office of the library director or before the city council. There is a profound silence, broken only by the imaginary chirping crickets, a pretty intimidating scenario as you set out to prove the senior department's worth. But you are prepared, and calmly open up your briefcase and are able to present the following elements (some can be in electronic format, but be prepared to give out takeaways):

- Neat reports and charts showing gradually increasing circulation statistics and patron use
- Wonderful graphs detailing growing attendance at programs and the usage of special services
- Senior department website hit counts and reports of patron participation
- Stacks of positive comments and solved negative ones
- A list of procured grants and how they have been successfully put to use
- Logs of program updates and changes with measures of success proven for each one
- A list of accomplished goals and corresponding outcomes met, including evidence of success
- A solid plan for the next fiscal year for reducing direct reliance on the library budget while expanding programming and/or services.
- An ambitious list of future departmental goals with objectives

You are able to accomplish this presentation all thanks to your constant and ongoing practice of evaluation. Will it be enough?

PROVING WORTH TO A WIDER AUDIENCE

The library board, the state senate, and voters may put you in the same position, but the difference is that they aren't all going to request a meeting giving you a chance to present your evidence. The only way to prove your worth to these all-important groups is by being incredibly active and dynamic with self-promotion and marketing.

- Transparency: Make all your evidence available online, taking into account privacy considerations for feedback commentary and photos. This can be via updates on a blog and Facebook or by creating content on your website featuring downloadable reports. Hard copies of yearly statistics should be always on hand at the reference desk.
- Show off the worth for all you're worth! Make sure the department blog and Facebook account is always going! Going! Going! Use it to highlight successful programs and services. Keep patrons connected and coming back for more through interactive features like videos, commentary, and forums. Be sure to have a "year in review" report posted onto the department blog or website. Highlight patron feedback as well as complaints and suggestions with solutions both in the library and online. Send out news articles on successful events, successful grant acquirements, and upcoming events to local newspapers and community gatekeepers.

- Get your name out there! This is most important, especially if you have a creative or fun name for your senior programs or senior department. Obtain a grant or use other funds to create creative and quirky signs of program pride. These can be bumper stickers, buttons, or even small posters featuring senior patron artwork. These tokens will be noticed by everyone in the community and might even become collectibles. What it really boils down to is this: the more your library and its programs and departments are out there in the world at large, the more they will be noticed by the people who have a voice in their ongoing life.
- Make your department and its programming so great (through lots of evaluation, hard work, effort, and spirit of enjoyment) that it's the place to be! If patrons feel like your department is a second home and family, you will be surprised by how hard they will fight for its survival.

CONCLUSION

Whether your library has taken the plunge to create a full-fledged senior department or simply put you in charge of creating some senior-specific programming, with this book you have in your hands the tools you need to accomplish it. We have endeavored to provide you with tips for creating and setting goals, provided you with our best ideas for creative premade programs and services, suggested dynamic ways to build a fan base and market, and finally offered a step-by-step how-to in the use of evaluation to prove your worth. The direction your library has taken in providing senior-specific programming is not only a valid and wonderful decision, but also very forward thinking. Senior patrons have long been ignored; by catering to them specifically, libraries can obtain many new valuable patrons and allies. Your new programming will no doubt be a work in progress, and, as it evolves, we hope our book provides you with continuous insights and help to spark your own great ideas. Let us know about your pitfalls and successes, and enjoy working with the most intriguing group of people we know—seniors.

APPENDIX A

ALA Guidelines for Library and Information Services to Older Adults

Library Services to an Aging Population Committee, Reference Services Section, Reference and User Services Association of the American Library Association 1987. Revised 1999, approved in 2008. Reprinted with permission.

INTRODUCTION

The American Library Association has a longstanding record of promoting library and information services to older adults. These guidelines, first developed in the 1970s, have been updated to respond to the changing demographics of an aging U.S. population. In 2007, one of every five persons was 55 years or older, or over 68 million people. The aging of the "baby boomers" will add to these numbers well into the next decade, and the lengthening of the average lifespan is creating several generations of older adults at a time that the U.S. has become more ethnically and linguistically diverse. As a result, the current population of older adults is the most heterogeneous in U.S. history. These updated guidelines reflect a basic principle in library services to older adults that recognizes this diversity and discourages stereotyping in planning collections, programs and services for this growing population.

For purposes of these guidelines, an "older adult" is defined as a person at least 55 years old.

The updating of these guidelines began in 2005. Current and past members of the Committee on Library Service to an Aging Population and the Office of Literacy and Outreach Services (OLOS) Library Service to the Aging Subcommittee contributed to this revision.

GUIDELINES FOR LIBRARY AND INFORMATION SERVICES TO OLDER ADULTS

1. Acquire current data about the older population and incorporate it into planning and budgeting.
    1.1.   Conduct surveys on a regular basis of the older population and the aging service providers in the community, including their numbers, demographic characteristics, and other information, such as their location and housing; educational, socioeconomic and ethnic background; religious organizations and other groups to which they belong; agencies that serve them; and the local media that targets older adults in the community.
    1.2.   Supplement surveys with focus groups and user studies among the community's older population to determine their needs and interests and to gauge how services, collections and programs might be made more appropriate and relevant to this population.
    1.3.   Collect data on the specific and varied information needs of older adults due to language, culture, education, income, Internet skills and access, gender identity/expression, sexual orientation, and age.
    1.4.   Utilize the above data in combination with the more general informational needs basic to older adults in their everyday lives. Such subjects include: health, health care, social security, financial planning, housing, independent living, elder law, caregiving (including grandparenting), lifelong learning (including adult literacy and computer skills), community service, civic engagement, and volunteering. The library's collections, programs, and informational services should reflect the diverse interests and needs of older adults.
    1.5.   Ensure that any services that target older adults are an integral and ongoing part of the library's operations and budget. Additional funding may be required for collections, accessibility equipment/ software, and the time expended by library staff in services to older adults and community. If a special grant or external funding is sought to support a pilot or demonstration program, consider how the program will be integrated into the library's regular budget and services at the end of the grant.
    1.6.   Involve older adults in the library's planning process by establishing an advisory committee. This committee might include older adults who are regular library users; library volunteers, staff, board members, or members of the library's Friends group; and leaders of organizations of older adults and other community organizations.
2. Ensure that the special needs and interests of older adults in your community are reflected in the library's collections, programs, and services.
    2.1   Appoint a librarian to act as a coordinator of services to older adults, ensuring that there is at least one designated staff member monitoring and developing the library's collections and services with older adults in mind.
    2.2   Consider how the library can be made more visible, more welcoming, and more relevant to older adult users.
    2.3   Advertise the library's services and website in local newspapers, magazines, radio or television programs that target older adults, and in senior centers, nutrition programs, and residential housing.
    2.4   Offer to speak to organizations of older adults about the library's services on a regular basis.
    2.5   Establish an ongoing liaison with agencies that serve older adults (especially senior centers that employ activity coordinators) to explore cooperative programming, recruit volunteers or friends of the library, and seek suggestions for programs or services that would encourage library use.
    2.6   Work with state library agencies that may provide staff training and development and information resources for older adults.

3. Make the library's collections and physical facilities safe, comfortable and inviting for all older adults.

    3.1   Evaluate your library's accessibility by older adults with physical, visual, aural, reading and other disabilities, according to the Accessibility Guidelines for Buildings and Facilities of the Americans with Disabilities Act.

    3.2   Consider providing at least one wheelchair in the library for public use.

    3.3   Accommodate users for whom prolonged standing is difficult by placing chairs or stools near stacks, information desks, check-out areas, computer terminals, and other areas. If possible, create a "Senior Space," using easy chairs gathered in an area adjacent to books and magazines of interest to older adults.

    3.4   Consider placing materials frequently used by older adults on easily accessible shelves.

    3.5   Place paperbacks, clearly labeled and well spaced, in areas of the library that are especially well lit, accommodating older adults who prefer paperbacks over heavier and more cumbersome hardback books.

    3.6   Assure that spacing between shelving accommodates users in wheelchairs.

    3.7   Ensure that signage is clear, Brailled (where appropriate), and readily visible to all, including users in wheelchairs. Library brochures should be in at least 14-point font type.

    3.8   Provide at least one computer station prominently labeled and installed with large type software for older adults with low-vision. If needs warrant and resources are available, acquire other assistive technology such as a stand-alone Reading Machine which speaks the book's text to a blind reader; speech synthesizer and related software; low-tech magnification and other devices.

    3.9   Provide TTY access, closed-captioned videotapes, and assistive listening systems to older adults with hearing disabilities.

    3.10 Acquire and make available books and periodicals in large print.

4. Make the library a focal point for information services to older adults.

    4.1   Cooperate with local Area Agencies on Aging, senior nutrition programs, senior volunteer programs, and others in the aging service provider network by advertising their service and making their publications and other information more readily accessible. The library can provide an invaluable service by organizing and consolidating information about government and community programs and services available to older adults.

    4.2   Consider developing or expanding the library's Web site to provide links to the sites of organizations of older adults, government departments and agencies serving older adults, newspapers and other Web sites whose focus is older adults.

    4.3   Ensure that the library's collection includes materials that are pertinent for caregivers of older adults, for their children or other family members, and for professional caregivers in the community.

5. Target the older population in library programming.

    5.1   Incorporate adequate funding for programs, materials, and services for older adults in the library's operating budget, and actively seek supplemental funding through partnerships with other agencies, organizations, and foundations interested in serving older adults.

    5.2   Plan programs each year that specifically target older adults and enhance their ability to remain independent and skillful library users. Publicizing such programs can heighten the library's visibility among the older population.

    5.3   Select themes for programs that deal with specific interests of older adults identified through user surveys, focus groups, or circulation statistics reflecting borrowing patterns by older adults.

    5.4   Plan programs for specific age groups or generations within the older population, being aware that interests and information needs vary greatly.

    5.5   Include intergenerational programs and participate in intergenerational projects sponsored by others in the community. Consider partnerships with local schools, daycare facilities or community organizations.

5.6   Pursue other opportunities for cooperative programming with partners such as community and senior centers; Area Agencies on Aging and other community agencies; and educational institutions offering continuing educational programs for older adults. Cooperative efforts might involve active participation in planning and delivering programs, assistance in advertising programs, or providing book displays and booklists in conjunction with the library's programs.

5.7   Consider providing computer and Internet courses specifically designed for older adults to accommodate a slower pace of instruction, provide sufficient time to develop "mousing skills," and allow for the possibility that some older adults may have visual, physical, or hearing disabilities. If possible, include individual tutoring provided by peers or others.

5.8   Explore opportunities to provide library services and programming to older adults outside the library, such as in senior or community centers, nursing homes, and senior housing units. Consider offering computer and Internet training in these locations.

5.9   Use library displays to combat ageism or the stereotypes in our society about older adults.

5.10   Provide opportunities for older adults to volunteer in the library.

5.11   Create opportunities for lifelong learning programs.

6. Reach out to older adults in the community who are unable to travel to the library.

6.1   Survey community needs and consider library budget planning to accommodate possible increases in demand for outreach services such as delivery of library materials by mail and mobile library services. Analyze community demographics, population forecasts, and housing trends to plan to meet this need effectively.

6.2   Offer the library's services to assistive living, alternative housing, senior day care, congregate meals sites, senior community centers, nursing homes and senior residential or care homes in the community. Also offer assistance to older adults who are confined to private residences or who are unable to carry library materials home.

6.3   Advertise the library's services through local media, public health agencies, and other agencies that work with older adults.

6.4   Eliminate waiting lists for library services through innovative approaches to delivery of materials, a redistribution of personnel, or establishment of a volunteer delivery system. Partner with Regional Libraries for the Blind and Physically Handicapped to expand available services.

7. Train the library's staff to serve older adults with courtesy and respect.

7.1   Provide sensitivity training to staff at all levels to make them aware of difficulties older adults may have in using the library, and how to make the library a more welcoming and comfortable place for older adults.

7.2   Train staff to recognize and combat ageism and stereotypes about older adults.

7.3   Ensure that all staff are aware of any special services the library offers that may be of interest to older adults, such as home delivery service, a talking books collection, a service to retrieve materials from the stacks, reading aids, or waiving of fines or fees.

7.4   Promote the employment of older adults as professional and support staff members.

8. Bibliography

Architectural and Transportation Barriers Compliance Board, (2002). *ADA Accessibility Guidelines for Buildings and Facilities (ADAAG)*. Retrieved June 6, 2008, from http://www.access-board.gov/adaag/html/adaag.htm

Association for Library Service to Children, American Library Association, (2004). "Books for Children Portraying Aging and Older Characters in a Positive Light." Retrieved June 6, 2008, from http://www.gwumc.edu/cahh/booklist/booklist_20041110.pdf

International Longevity Center–USA, New York, NY, (2006). *Ageism in America*. Retrieved June 6, 2008, from http://www.ilcusa.org/pages/publications/ageism-caregiving-sleep/ageism-in-america.php

Mates, Barbara T. (2003). *5-Star Programming and Services for Your 55+ Library Customers.* American Library Association, (ALA Programming Guides). Paperback.

Missouri State Library, Jefferson City, MO, (2002). *Serving Seniors: A Resource Manual for Missouri Libraries.* Retrieved June 6, 2008, from http://www.sos.mo.gov/library/development/services/seniors/manual/

Rubin, Rhea. (1993). *Intergenerational Programming, a How-To-Do-It Manual for Librarians.* Neal-Schuman Publishers, Inc.

APPENDIX B

Sample Surveys

ASSESSMENT SURVEY FOR OLDER ADULTS: CURRENT USERS

The _____ library is creating an older adult department from the ground up. Initial brainstorming envisions a unique space set aside just for older adults, including specialized services and programming and a concierge-style reference desk. Your thoughts and ideas are of utmost importance to us as we begin the planning process.

Please answer the following questions:

1. How did you hear about this survey?
2. How often do you come to the library?
3. What do you typically do at your library visits (check all that apply)
   - ☐ Check out book for self
   - ☐ Check out multimedia
   - ☐ Access our online resources
   - ☐ Bring another to use the library (i.e., grandchildren or friend)
   - ☐ Attend an event or program
   - ☐ Attend a class (computer skills, etc.)
   - ☐ Ask for a special service (i.e., research help)
   - ☐ Access the Internet
   - ☐ Browse
   - ☐ Pick up hold items
   - ☐ Use meeting/visiting space

4. How would you rate the following statements on a scale of 1–5?
   (1—Strongly disagree, 2—Disagree, 3—Agree, 4—Strongly agree, 5—N/A)
   I usually get what I need at the library.
   I have easy access to computer stations if I need one.
   I think the library is inviting.
   I think the restrooms are clean.
   I feel safe in the area surrounding the library.
   I feel safe in the library building.
   I am comfortable with the noise volume in the library.
   I am comfortable with the furnishing and seating areas in the library.

5. Do you use the library webpage? ☐ yes ☐ no
   If yes, how often and what for? If not, why?

6. What kinds of staff help are most important to you? (Choose up to two.)
   ☐ Reading recommendations
   ☐ Reference and research
   ☐ Job search
   ☐ Local history and genealogy help
   ☐ Access to government services (Medicare, social security)
   ☐ Instructional services (computer classes, resume classes)
   ☐ I prefer to find library resources on my own

7. If there was an area set aside for older adults just as there are for teens and children, would you give it a try? ☐ yes ☐ no

8. Which two of the following programming options are most important to you? (Choose up to three.)
   ☐ Activities and educational programs
   ☐ Literary events (author readings, book talks)
   ☐ Cultural events (music, film, dance, drama, or other arts)
   ☐ How-to topics such as consumer health, finance, and other instructional topics
   ☐ Civic engagement and current events presentations and discussions
   ☐ None of these are important
   ☐ Other _____

9. What program topic areas interest you most?
   (Examples: health, fitness, cooking, gardening . . .)

10. What is the ideal time of day for you to attend?

11. How do you spend your free time?

Please Tell Us More about Yourself . . .

- What is your gender? ☐ female ☐ male
- What is your age? ☐ 50–55, ☐ 56–60 ☐ 61–65 ☐ 66–70 ☐ 71–75 ☐ over 75
- Do you have any disabilities? ☐ yes ☐ no
  If so, please briefly describe:
- Are you able to get to the library on your own? ☐ yes ☐ no
- Do you have grandchildren you bring to the library? ☐ yes ☐ no
- Are interested in participating further in the planning process? ☐ yes ☐ no
  If yes, please provide us with your email or other contact information.

Thank you so much for your time! We are working hard to make the library a place for everyone in the community to enjoy, and we hope to see you soon!

ASSESSMENT SURVEY FOR OLDER ADULTS: CURRENT NONUSERS

The _____ library is creating an older adult department from the ground up. Initial brainstorming envisions a unique space set aside just for older adults, including specialized services and programming and a concierge-style reference desk. Your thoughts and ideas are of utmost importance to us as we begin the planning process. If you have never been to the library or it's been a long time, your feedback is extra important. It is vital to us that the library be a community gathering place that is used by all the members of the community. Our library is your tax dollars at work; by providing us with feedback, we can better make that money work for you.

Please answer the following questions:

1. How did you hear about this survey?
2. When was the last time you visited the library?
3. Why don't you use the library? (Check all that apply.)
   ☐ Library location
   ☐ Open hours and days
   ☐ Accessability/useability issue (like wheelchair access)
   ☐ Available selection of materials
   ☐ No need: I get everything I could get from the library elsewhere
   ☐ Other: _____
4. How to you meet your information needs? (Fill out any that apply.)
   • Books _____
   • Internet _____
   • Research _____
   • Meeting space _____
   • DVDs _____
   • Music _____
   • Community events _____
   • Classes _____
5. If there was an area set aside for older adults similar to the ones for teens and children, would you give it a try? ☐ yes ☐ no
6. Which of the following programming options would be most intriguing to you? (Choose up to three.)
   ☐ Activities and educational programs
   ☐ Literary events (author readings, book talks)
   ☐ Cultural events (music, film, dance, drama, or other arts)
   ☐ How-to topics like consumer health, finance, and other instructional topics
   ☐ Civic engagement and current events presentations and discussions
   ☐ None of these are important
   ☐ Other _____
7. What program topic areas interest you most?
   (Examples: health, fitness, cooking, gardening . . .)
8. What is the ideal time of day for you to attend?
9. How do you spend your free time?

Please Tell Us More about Yourself . . .

• What is your gender: ☐ female ☐ male
• What is your age? ☐ 50–55, ☐ 56–60 ☐ 61–65 ☐ 66–70 ☐ 71–75 ☐ over 75

- Do you have any disabilities? ☐ yes ☐ no
    If yes, please briefly describe:
- Are you able to get to the library on your own? ☐ yes ☐ no
- Do you have grandchildren you might bring to the library? ☐ yes ☐ no
- Are interested in participating further in the planning process? ☐ yes ☐ no

If yes, please provide us with your email or other contact information.

Thank you so much for your time! We are working hard to make the library a place for everyone in the community to enjoy, and we hope to see you soon!

SURVEY FOR COMMUNITY GATEKEEPERS

The _____ library is creating an older adult department from the ground up. Initial brainstorming envisions a unique space set aside just for older adults, including specialized services and programming and a concierge-style reference desk. Your thoughts and ideas are of utmost importance to us as we begin the planning process. It is vital to us that the library be a community gathering place that is used by all the members of the community. As a community partner or gatekeeper, your role allows you a unique perspective; please provide us some insight by answering the following questions:

1. What is your preferred method of contact from the library liaison?
2. What is your job position?
3. In what aspect do you have contact with older adults?
4. What is the population size of the older adult population that you have access to?
5. What do they have in common—that is, in what capacity does your organization work with older adults?
6. In your opinion, what are the most important things we could provide to your select group? (Check your top three.)
    - ☐ Reading recommends
    - ☐ Reference and research
    - ☐ Job search
    - ☐ Access to government services (Medicare, social security)
    - ☐ Mobile book services
    - ☐ Specialty services for disabilities
    - ☐ Entertaining programs
    - ☐ Educational programs (computer classes)
7. Which of the following programming options do you think would interest your group? (Choose up to three.)
    - ☐ Activities and educational programs
    - ☐ Literary events (author readings, book talks)
    - ☐ Cultural events (music, film, dance, drama, or other arts)
    - ☐ How-to topics such as consumer health, finance, and other instructional topics
    - ☐ Civic engagement and current events presentations and discussions
    - ☐ Other _____
8. Would you be willing to: (Please check all that apply.)
    - ☐ Pass out a survey to that group
    - ☐ Ask for volunteers for a focus group or personal interviews
    - ☐ Present at the library on your topic expertise
    - ☐ Become a possible member of our advisory council

ASSESSMENT SURVEY FOR LIBRARY STAFF

What if we created an older adult department from the ground up? Initial brainstorming envisions a unique space set aside just for older adults, including specialized services and programming and a concierge-style reference desk. Your thoughts and ideas are of utmost importance to us as we begin the planning process. Your current role, as a library staff member, allows you a unique perspective; please share your insights by answering the following questions:

1. What is your job position?
2. In your job duties here, do have contact with many older adults?
3. In your experience, what do you think older adults are looking for at the library? (Check your top three.)
   ☐ Reading recommends
   ☐ Reference and research
   ☐ Job search
   ☐ Access to government services (Medicare, social security)
   ☐ Mobile book services
   ☐ Specialty services for disabilities
   ☐ Entertaining programs
   ☐ Educational programs (computer classes)
4. What is your opinion on creating a specialized area set aside for older adults (akin to a children's or teen department)?
5. What are your main hobbies, skills, and interests—i.e., what are you knowledgeable or passionate about?
6. Would you be willing to be consulted with regarding collections on those topics?
7. Would you be willing to participate in programming on those topics?
8. Which of the following programming areas would you be interested in participating in? (Choose up to three.)
   ☐ Activities and educational programs
   ☐ Literary events (author readings, book talks)
   ☐ Cultural events (music, film, dance, drama, or other arts)
   ☐ How-to topics such as consumer health, finance, and other instructional topics
   ☐ Civic engagement and current events presentations and discussions
   ☐ Other _____
9. What kinds of programming, in your opinion, do you think older adults would like to attend?
10. Are there barriers that would keep these older adults from attending?
11. What is the best way to reach this group for marketing?
12. Do you have any additional ideas or suggestions?

APPENDIX C

Free Online Technology Tools

ASSESSMENT/EVALUATION

- **Form Spring**
  Website: http://www.formspring.me
  Create quick and fun survey questions that connect to social media such as your library's Facebook or Twitter account. Also works with a variety of blogging platforms such as Blogger, Wordpress, and Tumblr.

- **TooFAST**
  Website: https://www.toofast.ca
  This site is free for anyone to create an *online* assessment questionnaire. Multiple question formats can be created, and the site allows for an unlimited number of surveys to be completed. Their software automatically summarizes and consolidates on the Web or as XML.

- **My Survey Lab**
  Website: http://www.mysurveylab.com
  An online survey tool that allows up to 100 surveys to be sent for free. Includes analysis and reports.

- **Obsurvey**
  Website: http://obsurvey.com
  A free site that allows for complex assessment creations, including mandatory questions and branching questions. It can be plugged into your website and has a variety of reporting and download options. A great all-around tool for your survey needs.

- **Poll Daddy**
  Website: http://www.polldaddy.com

An online survey tool that allows up to 200 surveys to be sent for free per month, limited to 10 questions per survey. It includes basic analysis and reports. This is a great introduction to creating surveys.

- **Poll Everywhere**
  Website: http://www.polleverywhere.com
  Create a free poll with a 30 response limit. It can be imbedded in your website and is a great way to do a small trial run, but it won't be great for the long-term unless you purchase a more expensive account.

- **Survey Methods**
  Website: http://www.surveymethods.com/Index.aspx
  This one is a new favorite since they offer free professional accounts for nonprofits. You must apply first via their website at: http://www.surveymethods.com/academic-pricing.aspx
  Free accounts without the nonprofit deal are actually great as well since 20 max polls can be created with the ability to poll 500 recipients. They can be sent via your email list with an unlimited number of polls. The professional account has even more options, and it would be worth looking into for a large public library, especially if your library qualified for the free account.

- **Survey Monkey**
  Website: http://www.surveymonkey.com
  This site offers a great free account that includes 10 questions per survey but is limited to 100 responses per survey. They offer free templates and real-time results. The survey can be linked from your website or Twitter account or sent out via your email list.

- **Survs**
  Website: http://www.survs.com
  This site allows for 200 responses per survey and unlimited surveys that are 10 questions or fewer. You can link from your website or send via email to up to 100 contacts.

- **Zoho**
  Website: https://challenge.zoho.com/login.do
  Though mostly set up for creating school quizzes, this website could be enjoyable to use for fun challenge games. Their free account includes 100 tests. A fun idea would be to have a quiz before and after a program on the history of your area.

- **Zoomerang**
  Website: http://www.zoomerang.com
  Create unlimited surveys and polls from six basic templates with a limit of 12 questions and 100 responders. Send out via email, Facebook, Twitter, or your website. This is one of our favorites.

BLOGGING

This is a list of a few of our favorite blogging platforms. They are all free, but you can often upgrade to get your own domain name. (i.e., your blog name will no longer be followed by ".blogspot.com" or ".wordpress.com"). They all offer different templates and slightly different features. We recommend setting up a few to try out for your preferred ease of setup and use. If you have multiple employees, have them each create a blog via a different platform, and then you can test them out and make a decision based on their feedback as creators as well as your own as a user.

- **Blogger**
  Website: http://www.blogger.com
- **LiveJournal**
  Website: http://www.livejournal.com

- **Posterous**
    Website: https://posterous.com
- **TypePad**
    Website: http://www.typepad.com
- **Wordpress**
    Website: http://wordpress.org

BOOK CLUBS: ONLINE

The best way to get on board with promoting online book clubs is to do a survey or two. Find out if any of your staff are already using a program and which book clubs your patrons have heard of or maybe are already using. Then get to know that program and find out if it will work for your seniors. Next, it's time to promote it and get everyone involved.

- **Book Glutton**
    Website: http://www.bookglutton.com
    Create virtual reading groups, including social reading features such as live chat within a book.
- **Goodreads**
    Website: http://www.goodreads.com/
    This free site allows you to review what you have read, see what friends are reading, find new books, and even join book clubs and discussion groups.
- **LibraryThing**
    Website: http://www.librarything.com/
    If you have more than 200 books, this site has a fee, but it allows you to connect with the community at large, even making friends based on similar book interests.
- **Shelfari**
    Website: http://www.shelfari.com
    This free site allows you to create a virtual bookshelf, see what friends are reading, find new books, and learn more about your books. This is a great way for your patrons to connect to the library and to each other. It might even warrant a full activity program.

BOOKMARKING

You probably already know that creating a bookmark of a website records its address for later access. But you might not know that there are websites that keep track of all of your many bookmarks, allowing you to make, organize, and share lists of websites. These sites can also be helpful for patrons to learn about so they can keep organized for hobbies or research.

- **Delicious**
    Website: http://www.delicious.com
- **Diigo**
    Website: http://diigo.com
- **Google Bookmarks**
    Website: http://bookmarks.google.com
- **Yolink**
    Website: http://yolink.com

COLLABORATION

Use these great sites to work with other departments/senior centers/libraries to create cohosted events, programming, and large grant applications.

- **Conceptboard**
  Website: http://conceptboard.com
  This site gives you an online collaborative whiteboard space that can be used to share documents, drawings, spreadsheets, and so on. You can create drawings and diagrams from scratch or upload existing files. You can invite collaborators to share and discuss.
- **Google's Collaboration Tools**
  Website: http://www.google.com/apps/intl/en/edu/collaboration.html
  Google Docs, Google Sites, and Google Groups are free tools that are an easy-to-use part of online collaboration. Google Docs features real-time editing of shared documents. Everyone has access to the same working document, which is perfect for updating grant documents and creating large-scale programming. Google Groups features discussions and lists to help keep organized. Google Sites allows for permission-only websites, which can help keep track of progress and extra details for those involved.
- **Teamness**
  Website: http://www.teamness.com
  This great free program will probably be more than enough for what you need. While it's limited to 15 projects with 30 members, it features the ability to assign tasks to members in your team, message, comment, share whiteboards, and, best of all, be notified via RSS when there are changes.
- **Vyew**
  Website: http://vyew.com/content
  This site offers free teleconferencing and online meeting rooms featuring real-time desktop sharing—great for meetings with those coconspirators.
- **Wiggio**
  Website: http://www.wiggio.com
  This free site is hands down the easiest way to create collaborative groups. It features mass messaging, scheduling, file sharing and editing, polling, conference calling, video conferencing, virtual meetings, and project management tools. Work with other senior-dedicated department heads across the nation to create some magic.

COMPUTER MAINTENANCE

- **CCleaner**
  Website: http://www.pcworld.com/downloads/file/fid,24149/description.html
  This program cleans and optimizes your PC; it will clear out temporary files, erase browser histories, and more. *PC World* has many free approved tools like this.
- **Malwarebytes**
  Website: http://www.malwarebytes.org
  This free downloadable program can meet some of your antivirus needs and is useful for small or mobile library computers.

FACEBOOK AND ALTERNATIVES

- **Facebook**
  Website: www.facebook.com
  If you haven't heard of Facebook, it's time to dive in. This is the current premier site for social networking. Create a nonprofit account and get started.
- **Facebook for Beginners**
  Website: http://susan-ng.hubpages.com/hub/facebookforbeginners
  This is a great how-to guide for learning how to use Facebook.
- **Google+**
  Website: https://plus.google.com/up/start/?sw=1&type=st
  Google+ is a great new option for an alternative to Facebook that is rapidly gaining popularity. This might be a good choice for your department.
- **Google+ the Complete Guide**
  Website: http://mashable.com/2011/07/16/google-plus-guide
  This is a great how to guide for learning how to use Google+.

IMAGE EDITING WEBSITES

There is no better way to create your own branding than to create it yourself. Make your fliers and handouts interesting and fun by creating free artwork. You can also edit photos for inclusion on your website.

- **Aviary**
  Website: http://www.aviary.com
  Aviary offers a great set of image creation and editing tools. It provides tools for editing colors, size, and shadows and adding a variety of other effects to existing images. You can also create images such as logos from scratch.
- **FotoFlexer**
  Website: http://fotoflexer.com
  This a great site for creating a variety of effects, such as adding shapes, cropping, retouching, adjusting lighting, and doodling.
- **Gimp (aka GNU Image Manipulation Program)**
  Website: http://www.gimp.org
  A free image manipulation program, Gimp helps you accomplish tasks such as photo retouching, image composition, and image authoring. It can be used as a basic paint program, a higher level photo retouching program with some of the best Photoshop features, and even an image format converter. However, this is better for those who are more advanced in image manipulation.
- **Image Embellisher**
  Website: http://www.chami.com/html-kit/services/imge
  Image Embellisher is a simple tool for adding some unusual effects to your images.
- **Imageoid**
  Website: http://imageoid.com
  Imageoid offers a variety effects that you can apply to your image, such as changing an image from color to black and white.
- **IrfanView**
  Website: http://www.irfanview.com
  A great overall tool for cropping, resizing, and manipulating images.

- **LunaPic**

  Website: http://www.lunapic.com/editor

  Add over 200 effects to your images. This program includes a fun animation creator.
- **PicResize**

  Website: http://www.picresize.com

  PicResize has the option to resize single pictures or in a batch.
- **Picasa**

  Website: http://picasa.google.com

  A basic image editing tool, this program includes a built-in photo sharing feature.
- **Pixenate**

  Website: http://pixenate.com

  This site offers a basic image editing tool.
- **Psykopaint**

  Website: http://www.psykopaint.com

  Somewhat like an image editor combined with an art form, this site has very fun and interesting options for effects editing.
- **Splashup**

  Website: http://www.splashup.com

  A lot like the program Photoshop Elements, this site gives you all the basics in an easy-to-use format.
- **SumoPaint**

  Website: http://www.sumopaint.com/home

  This site is one of my favorites for creating interesting and unique paint-like projects. It contains many interesting tools for creating shapes and fills.
- **Resize Your Image**

  Website: http://www.resizeyourimage.com

  This site offers a simple tool for resizing images.
- **Shrink Pictures**

  Website: http://www.shrinkpictures.com

  This shrinks images that are in jpeg, gif, and png formats. It is a simple tool for resizing images.

IMAGE SHARING

These sites allow you to upload images to share with specific recipients or the general public. They are social sharing sites, and they can also be used to find images for presentations, such as staycation photographs on a variety of countries.

- **Behold**

  Website: http://www.behold.cc

  This site is a search engine for images with options to find images that can be downloaded to be modified and used commercially.
- **Flicker**

  Website: http://www.flickr.com

  Try searching for images using the license filter. That way you can find images that can be legally used in your marketing.
- **Photo Bucket**

  Website: http://www.photobucket.com

- **Picasa**
  Website: http://picasa.google.com
  Also an editing website, Picasa has an image sharing feature as well.

PODCASTING

A podcast is a great way to record upcoming events announcements. Patrons and community gatekeepers can then have an audio file that comes right to them via an RSS feed. Seniors can then listen to what's coming up right from their iPod or mp3 player. Podcasting is also a valuable tool for recording patron history stories. Usually you must have a microphone of some kind, but some offer phone-in recording.

- **Audacity**
  Website: http://audacity.sourceforge.net
  This is a great free audio editor.
- **Blabberize**
  Website: http://www.blabberize.com
  This site adds speech to an image. It has a feature that makes the mouth of the animal or person featured in an image open and close, just like it is really talking. Use it to help patrons create custom birthday cards for their friends.
- **Pod-O-Matic**
  Website: http://www.podomatic.com
  This site allows you to create free podcasts. A basic account is free!
- **Talkshoe**
  Website: http://www.talkshoe.com
  Talkshoe is a podcast and group phone presentation creator.
- **Voki**
  Website: http://voki.com
  Create speaking avatars and upload them to your website. Although more of a teaching tool, it can be used in the library to add some fun to your website.
- **Yodio**
  Website: http://www.yodio.com
  Yodio allows you to podcast by phone and add photographs.

PRESENTATIONS

Functioning similar to free versions of the program PowerPoint, these great presentation tools often contain easy-to-use features and extras.

- **Animoto**
  Website: http://animoto.com
  Animoto lets you create little music videos using images and music. Add URLs to give credit to your sources. Animato is a great way to create book trailers for new releases.
- **Empressr**
  Website: http://www.empressr.com
  Create quick presentations with photos, music, video, and audio. Then share your creations publicly or privately.

- **Slide Rocket**
  Website: http://www.sliderocket.com
  This alternative to PowerPoint includes a multitude of social media tools. For a price, it also features analytics to monitor who has viewed the slide and if they liked it. This might be a great go-to for creating an online program for patrons who can't attend the senior department library events. Since you can include video and social media tools, patrons can stay connected from their home or senior center.
- **Slide Share**
  Website: http://www.slideshare.net
  Here is a site to easily upload and share presentations and videos for free.
- **Squrl**
  Website: http://www.squrl.com
  Squrl allows you to create a playlist of videos from different Web sources to play all together later. This can be very handy when you want to create a presentation of a variety of Web videos and present them in a smooth, uninterrupted way.
- **Trip Wow**
  Website: http://tripwow.tripadvisor.com
  Trip Wow lets you create a travel video, with maps of your locations, featuring trip photos with locations—a great way to show places in the world. Find a staff member or patron who wants to show off his or her latest trip.
- **Tripline**
  Website: http://www.tripline.net
  This trip map is interactive and includes your own text and photos.
  For your travel series, create and save a collection of these, allowing patrons to upload their own to the senior website, and allow your patrons to explore the world.

TASKING AND TO-DO LISTS

- **Lazymeter**
  Website: http://www.lazymeter.com
  This site helps you track your tasks and those of your assistants and even measures your progress as you go.

TECHNOLOGY HELP

- **Bandwidth Planner**
  Website: http://etoolkit.org/etoolkit/bandwidth_calculator/about
  This site allows you to plan the computer setup for your senior department.

TEXT TO SPEECH

- **Expressivo**
  Website: http://say.expressivo.com
  Expressivo has a 200-word limit. The voices are wonderful and do a great job.

- **Talkr**
  Website: http://www.talkr.com
  Convert your blog to a podcast.
- **Vozme**
  Website: http://vozme.com
  This is a text-to-speech website. Instantly convert text to a downloadable mp3.

VIDEO CREATION AND EDITING

- **dVolver**
  Website: http://www.dvolver.com/live/moviemaker.html
  dVolver lets you create basic movies using their characters and backgrounds, along with bubble text. You must make the whole movie at once since you can't save and edit at a later time. This is a great way to present a funny informational video.
- **Fix My Movie**
  Website: http://www.fixmymovie.com/splash
  This site helps you clean up poor-quality movies.

- **Overstream**
  Website: http://www.overstream.net
  Overstream allows you to add captioning to streaming video. This is a must-have tool for a librarian in a senior department. This will help compensate for those who are hearing impaired.

VIDEO SHARING

Share your videos online. This is a great way to share longer movies that can't be uploaded to the senior website page.

- **Splicd**
  Website: http://www.splicd.com
  This site allows you to select and share simple segments of YouTube videos. Just note the start and end times and the videos' URLs. This is an incredibly useful site as you can cue up a bunch of video segments for presentation without needing to fast-forward or remember where to start and stop each video.
- **Vimeo**
  Website: http://www.vimeo.com
- **YouTube**
  Website: http://www.youtube.com

WEBSITE CREATORS

These are great for a number of reasons. If your library can't provide you with a department-specific site of your own due to space or IT issues, website creators are a must. Although free, most will feature ads unless you pay a nominal fee to remove them, often garnering your own IP address clean of their name at the same time along with other features, such as analytics.

- **Ahead**
  Website: http://ahead.com
  This site allows you to create layouts and publish via a free website. Similar to the Adobe program In Design, they do have paid options that include your own URL.
- **Google Sites**
  Website: http://sites.google.com/site/sites
- **Jimdo**
  Website: http://www.jimdo.com
- **Jottit**
  Website: http://jottit.com
  An extremely simplistic and easy-to-use website creator, Jottit allows you to create a site and have it up and running in seconds. You can embed images and video, but there are no fancy backgrounds or themes. This is bare bones.
- **Webs.com**
  Website: www.wcbs.com
  Create a simple to make, beautiful website, including a blog! This is my favorite website creator by far.
- **Weebly**
  Website: http://www.weebly.com
  Themes, drag-and-drop features, and blogging are all included.

APPENDIX D

Web Resource List

ASSOCIATIONS

AARP
  Website: www.aarp.org
National Council on Aging
  Website: http://www.ncoa.org/
  This organization provides a multitude of resources on a variety of topics.

CAREGIVING

Caregiver.org
  Website: http://www.caregiver.org/caregiver/jsp/home.jspFind resources by state to get assistance caring for a loved one or even yourself.
HelpStartsHere, "Caregiving"
  Website: http://www.helpstartshere.org/seniors-aging/caregiving
  Find a social worker: http://www.helppro.com/nasw/BasicSearch.aspx
National Association of Social Workers
  Website: http://www.socialworkers.org/
  This organization offers recommendations and resources for caregivers.
Parent Giving
  Website: http://bit.ly/ncEnLw
  Articles and resources on many topics related to elder care are available here.

The Senior Resource Network, "Surviving a Parent's Trip to the Hospital
   and Beyond: What to Know before You Go"
   Website: http://bit.ly/miIhhs

DEATH AND GRIEF: WIDOW/ER

National Hospice and Palliative Care Organization
   Website: http://www.nhpco.org
Widow Net
   Website: http://www.widownet.org
   A site to support widows and widowers.

ASSISTIVE TECHNOLOGY

JAWS Screen Accessibility Software
   Website: http://www.freedomscientific.com/products/fs/jaws-product-page.asp
   The JAWS software program reads aloud what is on the computer screen. JAWS is a bit pricy, but there is
   a free demo online, which can help you decide if this product is right for your library. JAWS also offers
   Braille output, converting the text on the computer screen to printed Braille.
Readability
   Website: http://www.readability.com/
   Free when activated while viewing a webpage, Readability allows seniors to see a decluttered version of
   the article they are viewing.
Zoom Text
   Website: http://www.aisquared.com/zoomtext
   Zoom Text allows patrons to easily enlarge any part of the computer screen. Zoom Text is software for
   purchase.

DISCOUNTS FOR SENIORS

AARP
   Website: http://www.aarp.org
Senior Discounts
   Website: http://www.seniordiscounts.com
   This site looks like a spam site, but don't be scared off.

EMPLOYMENT

AARP, "Work Search"
   Website: http://foundation.aarp.org/WorkSearch
Experience Works
   Website: http://www.experienceworks.org
   This site provides job training and employment for seniors.

National Council on Aging, "Mature Workers"
  Website: http://www.ncoa.org/enhance-economic-security/mature-workers
The Senior Community Service Employment Program (SCSEP)
  Website: http://www.doleta.gov/seniors
  This site helps seniors find work through paid training (in six states currently).

ESTATE PLANNING

AARP, "Estate Planning"
  Website: http://www.aarp.org/money/estate-planning
American Bar Association, "Estate Planning FAQs"
  Website: http://bit.ly/gEB9eg
Caring Connections
  Website: http://www.caringinfo.org
  This site also provides a direct link to download state-specific directives:
  Website: http://www.caringinfo.org/i4a/pages/index.cfm?pageid=3289
CNN Money, "Money 101 Lesson 21: Estate Planning"
  Website: http://money.cnn.com/magazines/moneymag/money101/lesson21
Elder Law Answers, "Estate Planning"
  Website: http://www.elderlawanswers.com/Elder_Info/Elder_Article.asp?id=703
New York Times, Your Money Guides, "Estate Planning"
  Website: http://nyti.ms/nC1U4F

FITNESS

Fitness Videos Geared toward Seniors
  Website: http://www.strongerseniors.com/
AARP Articles
  "9 Best Exercise Tips for Boomers": Website: http://aarp.us/fUPS7U
  "Water Works Aquatic Activity: A Painless Way to Stay Fit": Website: http://aarp.us/jEHGQU
American Senior Fitness Association, "Fitness Facts, Tips, and Handouts"
  Fitness Facts, Tips & Handouts
  Website: http://www.seniorfitness.net/sfafit.htm
DocStoc
  Exercises for poor posture in the elderly.
  Website: http://bit.ly/pLUDet
ElderGym
  Posture Exercises For Seniors and the Elderly: Website: http://www.eldergym.com/elderly-posture.html
  Correcting Bad Posture Exercises for Seniors and the Elderly: Website: http://www.eldergym.com/correcting-bad-posture.html
National Institute on Aging, "Exercise and Physical Activity: Your Everyday Guide from the National Institute on Aging"
  Website: http://www.nia.nih.gov/health/topics/exercise
Tai Chi Fitness, "Tai Chi Helps Senior Citizens Maintain Mobility"
  Website: http://taichifitness.info/tai-chi-helps-senior-citizens-maintain-mobility

FRAUD PREVENTION

Save and Invest.org
Website: http://www.saveandinvest.org/55Plus
This website includes free videos and info for older investors.

USA.gov, "Consumer Protection for Seniors"
Website: http://www.usa.gov/Topics/Seniors/Consumer.shtml
This site includes information on a variety of subjects from filing a compliant about a nursing home to finding your local consumer protection office.

AARP, "Fight Fraud"
Website: http://foundation.aarp.org/FightFraud

National Consumers League's Fraud Center
Website: http://www.fraud.org
This organization provides lists of great tips and advice sorted by types of fraud.

Investor.gov
Website: http://www.investor.gov
This website offers help on the following topics: fraud avoidance, understanding fees, and researching investment products and professionals.

Helping Seniors with Finances: How to Prevent Fraud
Website: http://www.youtube.com/watch?v=g90JZC-uUG8

Protecting Older Americans from Fraud
Website: http://www.youtube.com/watch?v=IJTPaKli3C0

GOVERNMENT

Administration on Aging
Website: http://www.aoa.gov

Supplemental Nutrition Assistance Program (Food Stamps)
Website: http://www.fns.usda.gov/snap
Eligibility: http://www.snap-step1.usda.gov/fns/

Department of Housing and Urban Development (HUD)
Website: www.hud.gov
Information for Seniors: Website: http://1.usa.gov/dYnKQn
HUD offers housing counselors and information on home ownership, foreclosure prevention, housing counselors, subsidized housing, and emergency homeowner loan programs.
State office locator: http://portal.hud.gov/hudportal/HUD?src=/states

Low Income Energy Assistance Program (LIHEAP):
Website: http://www.acf.hhs.gov/programs/ocs/liheap
This organization provides bill payment assistance, energy crisis assistance, and even weatherization and energy-related home repairs.

Meals on Wheels
Website: http://www.mowaa.org

Medicare
Website: http://www.medicare.gov
Website: http://www.cms.gov/home/medicare.asp
Here you can find doctors and learn more about your plan.

Medicare Rights Center (Nonprofit)
  Website: http://www.medicarerights.org
Making the Most of Medicare
  Website: http://www.youtube.com/watch?v=weExw8XHZCI
Medicare Rights Center
  Website: http://www.youtube.com/watch?v=Xol79ruB-lQ
Medicaid
  Website: http://www.cms.gov/home/medicaid.asp
Social Security Administration
  Website: http://www.ssa.gov
Lifeline across America
  Website: http://www.lifeline.gov/lifeline_Consumers.html
  This organization offers telephone assistance programs for low-income households, including help with starting and maintaining phone services.

GRANTS

AARP Foundation
  Website: http://www.aarp.org/aarp-foundation/Grants-Administration/
Administration on Aging, "Grant Opportunities"
  Website: http://www.aoa.gov/AoARoot/Grants/index.aspx
AstraZeneca Pharmaceuticals
  Website: http://www.astrazeneca-us.com/community-support
Atlantic Philanthropies
  Website: http://www.atlanticphilanthropies.org/search/grants
Cooperative Development Foundation
  Website: http://www.cdf.coop/applying-and-reporting
Grants.gov
  Website: http://www.grants.gov
  This site lists all federal grants.
Harry and Jeanette Weinberg Foundation
  Website: http://hjweinbergfoundation.org/grants/
Humana
  Website: http://www.humana.com/resources/about/corporate/hcb
Institute of Library and Museum Services
  Website: http://www.imls.gov/applicants/applicants.shtm
MetLife Foundation
  Website: http://bit.ly/uLnKK
National Endowment for the Arts
  Website: http://www.nea.gov/grants/index.html
National Endowment for the Humanities
  Website: http://www.neh.gov/grants/index.html
National Library of Medicine
  Website: http://www.nlm.nih.gov/grants.html
Pepsi Refresh Project
  Website: http://www.refresheverything.com

Picturing America Grant
  Website: http://picturingamerica.neh.gov
Robert Wood Johnson Foundation
  Website: http://www.rwjf.org/grants
The Foundation Center
  Website: http://foundationcenter.org
The Grantsmanship Center
  Website: http://www.tgci.com/funding.shtml
The Programming Librarian
  Website: http://www.programminglibrarian.org/library-grants.html
Verizon Grant
  Website: http://foundation.verizon.com/grant/guidelines.shtml
WellPoint
  Website: http://www.wellpointfoundation.org/home.html

LIBRARIAN RESOURCES

Free Management Library, "Basic Guide to Program Evaluation
  (Including Outcomes Evaluation)"
  Website: http://managementhelp.org/evaluation/program-evaluation-guide.htm
Transforming Life after 50
  Website: http://www.transforminglifeafter50.org/about
  This is a website full of resources for librarians catering to the 50+ age range. It includes statistics you could use to support the necessity of your department, including marketing ideas.
  Check out their section on program evaluation:
  Website: http://www.transforminglifeafter50.org/tools-ideas/assessment-evaluation
University of North Carolina Institute on Aging, "Lifelong Access Libraries Evaluation Project"
  Website: http://www.aging.unc.edu/programs/lal
  Be sure to check out their Centers for Excellence Final Report website: http://bit.ly/p6VmFP
Cleveland Public Library, "Seniors Connect"
  Website: http://www.cpl.org/Seniors.aspx
  Check out the wonderful senior site of a great public library.
Palo Alto City Library, "Feed Your Head" (Inspiration!)
  Website: http://paclboomers.blogspot.com/

MULTITOPIC SITES

50 Something
  Website: http://www.50something.us
  This website for members features articles, forums, a blog, and profiles with messaging and includes many great features, including a detailed travel section with reviews.
Love to Know Seniors
  Website: http://seniors.lovetoknow.com/Main_Page
  Information is provided for seniors and about senior topics on every subject from grants to health and fashion.

Wired Seniors
Website: http://www.wiredseniors.com/ageofreason
Wired Seniors offers forums, discussion boards, and thousands of links to senior websites.

RETIREMENT

AARP, "Retired and Loving It"
Website: http://aarp.us/haoEPj
Social Security, "How Should I Plan for Retirement?"
Website: http://www.ssa.gov/retirement
USA.gov, "Retirement"
Website: http://www.usa.gov/Topics/Seniors/Retirement.shtml
Wall Street Journal, **"Retirement 101: How to Figure out What You'll Need"**
Website: http://on.wsj.com/gaHVCc

SECOND CAREERS FOR SENIORS

AARP, "Work Search"
Website: http://foundation.aarp.org/WorkSearch
Experience Works
Website: http://www.experienceworks.org
FinAid
Website: http://www.finaid.org
A detailed website, it has information on how to find financial aid with many explanations, but it is not senior specific.
National Council on Aging, "Mature Workers"
Website: http://www.ncoa.org/enhance-economic-security/mature-workers/
The Senior Community Service Employment Program (SCSEP)
Website: http://www.doleta.gov/seniors
This site helps seniors find work through paid training (in six states currently).
U.S. News, **Money, "Forget Tuition: How Retirees Can Attend College for Free"**
Website: http://bit.ly/hXvLup
USA Today, **"Retired? Head Back to School with College Discounts"**

Website: http://usat.ly/aAlcqQ

TAXES

AARP, "AARP Foundation Tax-Aide"
Website: http://www.aarp.org/money/taxes/aarp_taxaide
To locate the nearest AARP Tax-Aide site, call 888-227-7669.
IRS, "Publications for Older Americans"
Website: http://www.irs.gov/individuals/retirees/index.html
For more information on the Tax Counseling for the Elderly (TCE) Program, call 800-829-1040.

USA.gov, "Money and Taxes for Seniors"
   Website: http://www.usa.gov/Topics/Seniors/Taxes.shtml

TECHNOLOGY

Generations Online
   Website: http://www.generationsonline.com
   This site provides free computer-use tutorials for seniors.

TRAVEL FOR SENIORS

AARP, "Travel"
   Website: http://www.aarp.org/travel
50 Something, "Destination Guides"
   Website: http://www.50something.us/modules.php?name=Travel
More with Less Today, "Travel Discounts for Seniors"
   Website: http://morewithlesstoday.com/travel-discounts-for-seniors
   This site lists major travel companies that offer a senior discount. It includes a detailed travel section with reviews by people over the age of 50.
Home Exchange 50 Plus
   Website: http://www.homeexchange50plus.com
Suite 101, "Senior Travel"
   Website: http://www.suite101.com/seniortravel
Travel with Grandma: Tips for Traveling with the Frail Elderly
   Website: http://www.travelwithgrandma.blogspot.com
USA Today, **"Travel Tips for the Elderly"**
   Website: http://traveltips.usatoday.com/travel-tips-elderly-13507.html

VOLUNTEERING

Peace Corps
   Website: http://multimedia.peacecorps.gov/multimedia/50plus/index.html
Senior Corps
   Website: http://www.seniorcorps.gov
Volunteer Abroad
   Website: http://www.volunteerabroad.com/search/seniors/volunteer-abroad-1
Volunteers of America
   Website: http://www.voa.org/Get-Help/National-Network-of-Services/Senior_Services

BIBLIOGRAPHY

American Foundation for the Blind. "Braille Technology." 2011. http://www.afb.org/Section.asp?SectionID=4&TopicID=31&DocumentID=1282 (accessed March 27, 2011). (Reprinted with permission, © 2011 American Foundation for the Blind. All rights reserved. This material originally appeared on AFB's website, http://www.afb.org.)

American Library Association, Library Leadership and Management Association. "Winners of the John Cotton Dana Library Public Relations Award." (Yearly since 2001.) http://www.ala.org/ala/mgrps/divs/llama/awards/johncottondanalibrarypublic.cfm.

American Library Association, Office for Literacy and Outreach Services. http://www.ala.org/offices/olos.

Cohen, Gene D. *The Mature Mind: The Positive Power of the Aging Brain.* New York: Basic Books, 2006.

Cornog, Martha, Joseph McPeak, and Tracey Ray. "The Free Library of Philadelphia's Senior Center: Comfy and Stimulating." *Public Libraries* 49, no. 5 (September/October 2010): 45–50. Library Literature and Information Science Full Text Database, WilsonWeb (accessed August 22, 2011).

Day, Jennifer Cheeseman. "National Population Projections." U.S. Census Bureau, 2011. http://www.census.gov/population/www/pop-profile/natproj.html (accessed March 19, 2011).

Dempsey, Kathy. *The Accidental Library Marketer.* Medford, NJ: Information Today, 2009.

Dowd, Nancy, Mary Evangeliste, and Jonathan Silberman. *Bite-Sized Marketing: Realistic Solutions for the Overworked Librarian.* Chicago: American Library Association, 2010.

Federal Interagency Forum on Aging-Related Statistics. *Older Americans 2008: Key Indicators of Well-Being.* Washington, DC: U.S. Government Printing Office, 2008. http://www.agingstats.gov/Main_Site/Data/2008_Documents/OA_2008.pdf ((accessed March 18, 2010).

Foster-Bey, John, Robert Grimm Jr., and Nathan Dietz. "Keeping Baby Boomers Volunteering: A Research Brief on Volunteer Retention and Turnover." Corporation for National and Community Service, 2007. http://www.nationalservice.gov/pdf/07_0307_boomer_report.pdf (accessed April 2011).

Horovitz, Bruce. "Big-Spending Boomers Bend Rules of Marketing." *USA Today,* 2010. Newspaper Source, EBSCOhost (accessed August 22, 2011).

Joseph, Mylee. "Active, Engaged, Valued: Older People and Public Libraries in New South Wales." *Australasian Public Libraries and Information Services* 19, no. 3 (September 2006): 113–17. Library Literature and Information Science Full Text Database, WilsonWeb (accessed August 22, 2011).

Kerico, J. "Westminster Village: A Theme-Based Approach to Teaching Seniors about the Internet." *Indiana Libraries* 25 no. 3:9–12 (2006). Library Literature and Information Science Full Text Database, WilsonWeb (accessed April 18, 2010).

McDonald, Maureen. "Library Makeovers Draw Seniors: Public Places Aim to Become Inviting Senior Spaces, Offering Wii as well as Books." *AARP Bulletin,* 2011. http://www.aarp.org/personal-growth/life-long-learning/info-05-2011/library-makeovers-draw-seniors.html (May 16, 2011).

National Institute on Aging and the National Library of Medicine. "Making Your Website Senior Friendly, March 2009." http://www.nia.nih.gov/HealthInformation/Publications/website.htm (May 8, 2011).

New Media Consortium. *The Horizon Report.* 2011. http://net.educause.edu/ir/library/pdf/HR2011.pdf (accessed February 10, 2011).

Rossi, Lisa. "Howard County Library Will Loan Nook E-Readers." *Columbia Patch,* October 2010. http://columbia.patch.com/articles/howard-county-libraries-will-loan-nook-e-readers (accessed May 16, 2011).

Rothstein, Pauline M., and Diantha D. Schull. *Boomers and Beyond: Reconsidering the Role of Libraries.* Chicago: American Library Association, 2010.

Strauch, Barbara. *The Secret Life of the Grown-Up Brain: The Surprising Talents of the Middle-Aged Mind.* New York: Viking, 2010.

Swinson, Judy Looman. "Focusing on the Health Benefits of Volunteering as a Recruitment Strategy." *International Journal of Volunteer Administration* 24, no. 2 (2006). http://www.ijova.org/PDF/VOL24_NO2/IJOVA_VOL24_NO2_Swinson%20_FocusingontheHealthBenefits.pdf (accessed April, 2011).

Tsai, J. "Marketing Knows No Age Limit." *DestinationCRM.com,* October 20, 2009. http://www.destinationcrm.com/Articles/CRM-News/Daily-News/Marketing-Knows-No-Age-Limit-57551.aspx (accessed April, 2011).

USA Today. "Aging Boomers Strain Cities Built for the Young." 2011. http://yourlife.usatoday.com/health/ story/2011/07/Aging-boomers-strain-cities-built-for-the-young/49175380/1 (accessed July 2011).

Walters, Suzanne. *Marketing: A How-to-Do-It Manual for Librarians*. New York: Neal-Schuman Publishers, 1992.

Williamson, K., M. Bannister, and J. Sullivan. "The Crossover Generation: Baby Boomers and the Role of the Public Library." *Journal of Librarianship and Information Science* 42, no. 3 (2010): 179–90.

INDEX

ABOUT THE AUTHORS

ANN ROBERTS is the Continuing Education Consultant for the Missouri State Library. In that capacity, she plans training opportunities for library workers in the state of Missouri, including trainings in services to seniors and special populations, and serves as the coordinator of the Missouri Center for the Book. She is a former member of the Academy of Certified Archivists, a member of the Missouri Library Association, and has published two other books in the Crash Course series, *Crash Course in Library Services to People with Disabilities* and *Crash Course in Library Gift Programs: The Reluctant Curator's Guide to Caring for Archives, Books, and Artifacts in a Library Setting*.

STEPHANIE G. BAUMAN is a Master of Library Science graduate of San Jose State University. She was inspired to be a part of this book by her late aunt, Cathy Tice, who volunteered with pizzazz and enthusiasm at her local senior center. She is an active blogger, reviewing books for recommendation to school library collections. Stephanie is the author of *Storytimes for Children,* also published by Libraries Unlimited.

CPSIA information can be obtained at www.ICGtesting.com
Printed in the USA
LVOW09s1445051213

364045LV00017B/737/P